"A very readable, genuinely intelligent, and highly resourceful book. A worthy read!"

—**Alan Hirsch**, author of *The Forgotten Ways*; founding director of Forge Mission Training Network

"Provocative and practical at the same time. A must read for all who yearn for a unified and healthy body of Christ in a connected world."

—**Dr. Mary Kate Morse**, professor of leadership and spiritual formation and associate dean, George Fox Evangelical Seminary; director of strategic planning, George Fox University

"A treasure chest of insights to further the conversation on the nature of the missional church in post-Christendom Western societies."

—**Eddie Gibbs**, author of *ChurchMorph*; senior professor of church growth, Fuller Theological Seminary

"Interesting and fascinating. . . . You may never look at 'church' the same way again."

—**John R. Franke**, Clemens Professor of Missional Theology, Biblical Seminary; author of *Manifold Witness: The Plurality of Truth*

"Inventive, theological, and profoundly challenging. I recommend it to all Christians emerging in this inescapable cultural reality."

—**David Fitch**, B. R. Lindner Chair Evangelical Theology, Northern Seminary; Reclaimingthemission.com

"Friesen brings together current thinking on the Trinity, the kingdom of God, and the missional church, and creates the first contextual ecclesiology for a networked world. Highly recommended."

—**Ryan Bolger**, associate professor of church in contemporary culture, Fuller Theological Seminary; co-author of *Emerging Churches*

"A wonderful tutorial for those who want to experience the kingdom as more than a wistful idea."

—**Reggie McNeal**, missional leadership specialist for Leadership Network

 **ēmersion**

Emergent Village resources for communities of faith

www.emersionbooks.com

Thy
Kingdom
Connected

What the Church Can Learn from Facebook, the Internet, and Other Networks

Dwight J. Friesen

BakerBooks

a division of Baker Publishing Group
Grand Rapids, Michigan

Published by Baker Books
a division of Baker Publishing Group
P.O. Box 6287, Grand Rapids, MI 49516-6287
www.bakerbooks.com

Printed in the United States of America

Library of Congress Cataloging-in-Publication Data
Friesen, Dwight J., 1969–
    Thy kingdom connected : what the church can learn from facebook, the internet, and other networks / Dwight J. Friesen.
        p.   cm.
    Includes bibliographical references.
    ISBN 978-0-8010-7163-8 (pbk.)
    1. Interpersonal relationships—Religious aspects—Christianity. 2. Online social networks. 3. Social networks—Computer network resources. 4. Church. I. Title.
    BV4597.52.F75 2009
    231.7′2—dc22   2009030229

Map of Washington State on page 42 appears courtesy of the Washington State Department of Transportation.

Map of flight routes on page 42 appears courtesy of Alaska Air/ Horizon Air.

09   10   11   12   13   14   15   7   6   5   4   3   2   1

To Lynette and Pascal,
who make the world a more beautiful place

ēmersion is a partnership between Baker Books and Emergent Village, a growing, generative friendship among missional Christians seeking to love our world in the Spirit of Jesus Christ. The ēmersion line is intended for professional and lay leaders like you who are meeting the challenges of a changing culture with vision and hope for the future. These books will encourage you and your community to live into God's kingdom here and now.

Drawing on emergence thinking, network theory, and a fascination with the new sciences, Dwight Friesen gives us important new ways to speak of the kingdom of God: relational, reconciling, and connective. It is, he says, a linked, scale-free network of "differentiated unity." *Thy Kingdom Connected* is intended to encourage us to live in the Jesus way as a journey, gathering fresh definitions and fascinating metaphors. But even more that that, we arc infected with a hopeful vision of an exciting future.

ēmersion

Emergent Village resources for communities of faith

Contents

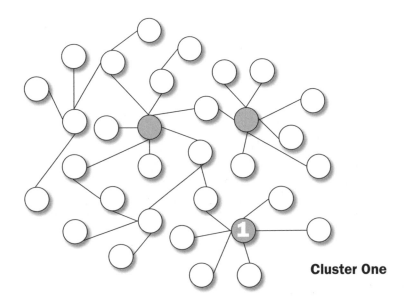

Cluster One

Seeing Connectively

This first cluster of chapters explores our need for seeing more connectively. Dr. Leonard Sweet's foreword beautifully draws us to consider God's connective creation. We will peer into the life and ministry of a pastor seeking a more relationally connective way of leading a local church. Then we will briefly survey our cultural context to better understand how our atomized vision has been formed, setting the stage for the rest of the book.

Foreword

Let There Be Links

The Bible begins with God busy for a bit, creating heavens and earth, darkness and wind. But the first sounds of creation, God's first words, are these: "Let there be light" (Gen. 1:3). Some say these words were sung rather than said. But whether sung or said, light was the first creation. When the One-in-Three God wanted company in the universe, God created light. The unknown became known. And with dispatch God carefully separates this light from the "dark." Because of that divine "Let there be light" word or song, there is no longer a "void." Instead "there was evening and there was morning, the first day" (Gen. 1:5). God's design unfolds and gets underway.

Today we know a lot about light. We know the speed at which it travels (186,000 miles/second, or 671 million miles/hour). We know it comes on when we insert a plug or throw a switch. We know it describes potato chips that taste really bad.

But the most important thing we know about light is what makes light "light," and that is links. Light only comes about through links, through relationships. Interlinked frequencies communicate and emit different kinds of light—ultraviolet, infrared, a rainbow spectrum of colorful relationships. Light is formed by the connection between frequencies, the relationship between particles. The links give us the light that transforms our world. Maybe a better translation of "Let there be Light" is, "Let there be links."

We see God as light because the links are what connect us to the Triune link. In the Christian tradition, revelation is understood as an experience of light. Light is God's self-communication. The difference between "God is nowhere" and "God is now here" is but the addition of a link, a span of relationships.

What makes darkness so terrifying is that we can no longer see things in their relationships. Everything appears delinked. Has there ever been a child who has never been afraid of the dark? We've always told our kids this double-edged "good news": "There is nothing that exists in this world that isn't present both in the dark and in the daylight." For kids that is supposed to mean there are no magical creatures that only appear to terrorize children at night. For parents that message serves to remind us we must always be on our guard.

But there is definitely an inborn, universal "fear of the dark." Why is there a fear of this blanket of blackness?

Because we were made to link with God. Many say John 3:16 is the most perfect encapsulation of the good news of the gospel: "For God so loved the world that he gave his only son, so that everyone who believes in him may not perish but may have eternal life."

It is good news. It is the best news. But it is not the only news. The news is not just that God loves the world. The news is not just that because of this love God gave his Son. This news also reports that "everyone who believes in him" may enter and enjoy a new kind of linkage, a link called "eternal life."

But wait a minute: the "good news" has a qualification.

To demonstrate what this new, extraordinary relationship entails, John's gospel immediately goes back to the competing images of "darkness" and "light." Those "in darkness" are not "in him." Those who live in the light are "in God." Light is created out of relationships. Light is about links. A life lived according to the light, "in the light," a life lived "in God," is a life lived in relationship with God.

A life lived in the dark is the opposite, not because the dark is bad or evil, but because we can forget in the dark the links of the light. We do "evil," or morally ambiguous things "at night," because in the darkness we feel we can delink, we can become disconnected to the rest of the relationships in our lives.

Nowhere understands this moral truth quite so well as Las Vegas, which has come up with a perfect twenty-first century rendition of John 3:19–21: "What happens in Vegas, stays in Vegas." In the city that is known for going and flowing in the dark, "What happens in Vegas, stays in Vegas" is a slogan that pretends that what happens in the dark does not impact our "real" lives—our relational lives, our "link" lives.

But like we tell our kids, everything that exists in the daylight *is* there in the dark, and everything that happens in the dark is still present in the daylight. We cannot escape our knowledge of good and evil and delink from God or from each other. We cannot pretend to be one thing in the daylight and another in the darkness.

The greatest delusion of the dark is this: that you can delink from everyone else, that you are the center of the universe. The dark can turn the "universe" into a "*you*-niverse." In this universe, you think that you are all that matters, that everything that exists is there to meet your needs. In the dark, without points of reference outside yourself, you start to think that nothing matters beyond your desires. When only what you want matters, there is total disregard for every other person, as well as the planet. It is not enough to say that this Las Vegas "youniverse" has mistaken the search for personal fulfilment with the search for God. It is more accurate to say that in this delinked, dark, narcissistic culture, we have come to think of ourselves as gods who are entitled to whatever we want, everyone and everything else be damned.

No wonder this Youniverse is filled with narcissists who see themselves as the navel of the universe.

No wonder this Youniverse is filled with solipsists who are totally in love . . . with self . . . and who can't see anybody else but themselves.

No wonder this Youniverse is filled with goddifiers who trust not in the God of heaven and earth, but in the god of themselves. Everything is permitted, nothing is taboo, anything goes in the pursuit of calling out your name in the dark.

No wonder this Youniverse is filled with islanders who choose to do the two worst things you can do in life: refuse to link, and refuse to be linked.

No wonder this Youniverse is filled with Las Vegans who do "what is right in their own eyes."

Oh, by the way, this Youniverse is the biblical definition of hell: John 3:16, God's love of this world, requires of us John 3:21, for us to come into the light.

We have a choice: let there be light, let there be links. Or . . .

Let there be Las Vegas. Let there be a delinked Youniverse.

Dwight Friesen's marvelous study of a linked universe reminds us of this fundamental "Let-there-be-links" question: When does night become day?

The answer? When you can look into a person's eyes and see a brother or sister.

The answer? When you can see the links.

Leonard Sweet
Drew University, Madison, New Jersey
George Fox University, Portland, Oregon

Preface

One Pastor's Quest for a More Connective Way

Something is on the way out and something else is painfully being born. It is as if something were crumbling, decaying and exhausting itself, while something else, still indistinct, were arising from the rubble. . . . We are in a phase when one age is succeeding another, when everything is possible.[1]

Václav Havel

Renee has a love/hate relationship with the church. Some of her fondest memories, life-shaping moments, and deep relationships have been within the body of Christ. She entered pastoral ministry with a deep sense of calling to participate with God in connecting people to life in the way of Christ, to meaning and tradition, and to engage this work with a heart for reconciliation. Over the years she has had a front row seat to a spectacular divine drama: breathtaking redemptive narratives, broken relationships reconciled, grief embraced, hope discovered, and so on.

Her front row seat also permitted her to witness the horror of the "bride of Christ" morph into the "bride of Frankenstein," wreaking havoc on those in its path. Annual meetings that went sour, cruel unsubstantiated rumors spread throughout the body, declining numbers, shrinking budgets, and the sinking feeling that she simply wasn't good enough. She had come to dread random phone calls

15

from parishioners wanting to speak with her, fearing that they too were about to tear away yet one more strip of her dwindling dignity. When she attended conferences or read of "successful" churches, she often wondered how those leaders were wired, how they were able to be relationally connected in the detailed lives of the people in their churches. Renee used to love being with people and now she increasingly saw them as interruptions.

When she and her husband, Doug, left seminary, they would often talk and dream late into the night with anyone who would listen about the wonder and beauty of doing life together. They dreamed of running their church like a finely oiled machine; of being known and knowing others; of participating in the day-to-day life of their neighborhood as they let the light of Christ shine through them. They dreamed about bearing with one another, loving through dis-agreements, and finding small, practical ways to demonstrate their love for Christ by loving the members of their church family and beyond. They knew that "tune-ups" would be necessary from time to time, and saw such maintenance as part of their calling.

Five years into their first pastorate, those passionate late-night con-versations were a distant memory. "Youthful idealism, borderline uto-pianism," she said to comfort herself. Words like *defensive*, *exhausted*, *stale*, *scared*, *dry*, and *alone* were now regularly appearing in her journal. Doug was also growing disillusioned with Renee's vocational ministry. He subtly dreaded board meeting nights. He watched Renee return home with mixed feelings, sometimes feeling misunderstood and often not understanding. He knew it was becoming too much for him. He had started to go to bed before she returned just so he wouldn't have to see the discouragement on her face. Sometimes he even faked sleeping. After five years she and Doug were done. "Forget 'tune-ups'!" said Renee. "We've crashed and burned; it's a write-off. We're just lucky to be able to walk away." Renee submitted her resignation with nowhere to go; maybe she could work with Doug's dad.

While packing up her study—and her dreams—she came across a binder filled with essays she had written in grad school. A wave of nostalgia washed over her as she sat flipping the pages, reading a para-graph here and there. She thought of some of her professors, her fellow students, and the passion she had once lived and breathed. "What a far cry from this," she thought, looking at her boxed up life.

When Renee found the essay she had written on Bonhoeffer's *Life Together*,[2] she read the entire thing through—twice—with glossy eyes. "What has gone wrong *here*?"

Working with Doug's dad was okay. Renee liked to joke that she went from hocking "eternal fire insurance" to auto insurance, rarely eliciting more than a slight chuckle. She and Doug had a hard time finding a church to attend, so for a while they quit going altogether. For the first time in their lives, they slept in on Sunday mornings, and they liked it.

As Renee and Doug talked with the people they were meeting in their new life, they were surprised at how many connected with their story. Their feelings of being disappointed or hurt by the institutional church found ready "Amens" as did the sense of new freedom in their postchurch life.

- "Since I quit 'going to church,' I have more time with my family, and I love it."
- "Now that I don't have committee meetings, I'm getting to know my neighbors. And it feels like they actually want to know me."
- "Today, when I hear of a financial need or I see a friend who needs help, I give; I don't need to wait for a 'church response.' I am the response."
- "Since I 'dropped out' of Sunday school and midweek programs, our family has started to volunteer one Saturday each month at a neighborhood food bank. We're making a real difference, and I think Christ is pleased."
- "My husband and I go for walks on Sunday mornings. We talk and pray. And we're no longer content with Christian clichés; instead we wrestle with God—together."

Renee and Doug began to ask hard questions of their previous experiences of church and began to find others seeking a new vision for life and church. They started a small group in their home. Often their conversations were as profane as they were prophetic. They argued over the church's hierarchical power structures and wondered whether truly flat systems were possible. If so, what might that mean for the function and role of leaders? They debated what success looks like for a faith community and wondered whether it would be possible for a community to develop programs for holistic spiritual transformation. They even wondered about the ethics and theology of marketing churches, imagining what it might look like for a community of faith to be known for its love more than its slick door hangers. One of the questions that kept resurfacing for them was what they called the "myth of the priesthood of all believers": the disproportionate amount of money spent on buildings and religious professionals, and how so much church growth seemed to stem from clergy's instinctive grasp at self-preservation.

Their conversations left no stones unturned and there was a clear and deep longing to participate with God in the re-creation of all things. Their conversations often took them back to Christ's interactions with the religious leaders of his day. Jesus's ministry was so relational. He had such authority but refused to wield power. There was little or no discernible program; he instead met each person uniquely.

After a while God's Spirit began to challenge Renee, Doug, and their small group. They began to sense that they could do more than simply criticize what they had experienced; through their hurts God might actually be inviting them to begin something imaginative, something constructive. Maybe their little cluster of kingdom-oriented friends were seeing a more "networked" form of church emerge—a faith community marked by a different kind of structure, without dogmas of exclusion but with open doors of invitation; a community where power was given away, and life could flourish.

> The ability to perceive or think differently is more important than the knowledge gained.[3]
>
> David Bohm

Seeing the Problem as Seeing the Solution

The ache felt by pastors like Renee and the questions echoing in the hearts and minds of people like her and her little community are the questions we will explore in *Thy Kingdom Connected*. The great challenge facing many of our families, organizations, and churches today is that we do not see relationally. We've lost sight of God's networked kingdom. We need corrective lenses.

Our vision has been deceived by the illusionary atomizing notion of the "self," duping us into thinking that we don't need others; or that it's "us" against "them"; or that only one can win; or a host of other similar illusions that are equally insidious and equally counter to the gospel of Jesus Christ. In contrast with God's clear vision in which everything belongs, in whom the reconciliation of all things is possible, and where the re-creation of all is already underway, our vision often causes us to see ourselves as being alone. Sometimes our modern, individualistic vision even encourages us to see ourselves as victimized by "them," robbed of what is truly "ours." Failure to see the interconnections of the world created by God can only result in "di-vision." We need a fresh vision of God's networked kingdom.

At the height of modernity we saw individuals; we saw separate organizations and standalone institutions; and we actually thought that when we split an atom, a church, or a marriage, the relationship ended. Today we know that we were mistaken. We are seeing with increasing poignancy that separation and division is not the deepest truth of life. Rather, we are beginning to see that underneath the guise of division is an even deeper connection that cannot be severed. This deeper connection links all of humanity, even all of creation, together in and through its Creator. Some call it the "web of life"; others call it "Gaia"; and Jesus revealed it as the "kingdom of God." This is a quantum leap in our understanding of life as relational: it provides a meaningful articulation of the deepest truths of life that we have always known to be true in experience.

And so there is great hope on the horizon. Jesus encouraged us by saying, "Whoever has ears to hear, and eyes to see . . ." (Luke 10:10–17). Well, like a great awakening of sorts, people from every corner of the globe, from multiple academic disciplines, from every ecclesial tradition, are rediscovering ancient ways of perceiving these interconnections. And for many, the use of newer social networking technologies are enlivening imaginations for connective living.

The goal of this book is very simple. I want it to reorient the way we see the world. Where we once saw division, *Thy Kingdom Connected* will equip us to see an opportunity for reconciliation;

where we once saw disconnection, our imaginations will be open to missionally linking . . . you get the idea.

Thy Kingdom Connected presents a relationally connective paradigm of God's networked kingdom that will better enable you and me to see God, humanity, and all of creation as being interconnected. And when this relational paradigm, this hermeneutic, is applied to the study and praxis of ecclesiology, the people of God will be better prepared to live into the *image of God*, thus incarnating the *mission of God*. Within these pages you will see a vision of God's networked kingdom and the glorious beauty of the indigenous, localized kingdom expressions that are the churches interconnected in God's glorious tapestry.

> The question is not what you look at—but how you look and whether you see.[4]
>
> Henry David Thoreau

Recommended Resources for Further Reflection

Walter Truett Anderson, *All Connected Now: Life in the First Global Civilization* (Cambridge, MA: Westview Press, 2001).

Jürgen Moltmann, *The Trinity and the Kingdom* (Minneapolis: Fortress Press, 1993).

Questions for Personal Reflection or Small Group Conversation

- Where did you find resonance in Renee and Doug's story?
- Describe one of the seasons in your life when you experienced a deep sense of connectedness.
- What are some of the questions or concerns that you have regarding church life as you have experienced it? How might your question or concern be an invitation to imaginatively lean into a more relational way of being?
- As you read Scripture and look at Jesus and his followers, what are your hopes for doing life in community for the sake of the world?

Introduction

Improving Our Connective Sight by Readjusting Our Lenses

The real voyage of discovery consists not in seeking new landscapes, but in having new eyes.[1]

Marcel Proust

We're a decade into the twenty-first century and many church leaders are scrambling to figure out why the systems we have built seem to be producing results counter to flourishing life. Many are wondering why so many churches and denominations are in decline when they are proclaiming the gospel. Why are poles of the church seemingly becoming more polarized? Why are so many leaders less fulfilled as individuals, and why is our experience of community seemingly diminished? Why are our "tried-and-true" ways of being the church not producing the flourishing life they once did? What has changed?

The church is not alone in struggling with these crises. Politicians, ecologists, economists, educators, corrections officers, social activists, and many others are encountering a whole series of personal, local, national, and global problems. These problems threaten not only human life but the life of most species on our planet. But the good news in all of this is that problems are opportunities for grace to be evidenced; it is in the face of failure and seemingly impossible challenges that new ways of seeing are born. Now is such a time.

The more we explore the significant challenges of our time, the more we are coming to realize that they cannot be understood as being isolated from each other. There is no single solution to the complexity of the challenges we face. No church growth conference, no missional book, no verse of Scripture can alone be our guiding light. We have systemic problems, which is to say the problems facing the church and all of humanity are a series of interconnected, interanimating, and interdependent problems.

Consider the growth of the sex trade industry, which has always been part of human experience but now seems especially prevalent. The sex trade industry is fueled in part by cultures that have virtually no restraints on the pursuit of personal pleasure and are less reflective about the impact of "my pursuits" on others. It is further energized by easy access to pornography, the low cost of global travel, and the growing divide of the world's poorest and richest, making it more difficult than ever for the poorest of the poor to earn enough money to care for their families. The solution to ending the sex trade cannot rest in passing a lone law, or in simply rescuing sex slaves or prosecuting offenders.

Or think of the film by Davis Guggenheim, *An Inconvenient Truth*, which highlights global climate change and Al Gore's efforts to bring this issue to the public consciousness. The movie makes clear that there is no singular, quick answer; after all, if there were, it wouldn't be an issue.

In a very important way, these two mammoth global issues are fueled by the problem this book addresses: a crisis of perception. This crisis of perception stems from the reality that most of us—and especially our institutions, churches, and seminaries—subscribe to a view of the world that is not only outdated but is also theologically shallow. The time has come for us to reflect on the complexity and the interdependency of all aspects of created life. Our Christian narrative begins with a personal, Triune God who creates heaven and earth, a God in whom all that lives finds breath and movement and being. All that exists finds wholeness in its connection to God. Any perception of the world that suggests or reinforces the notion that individual decisions, beliefs, and actions have little or no bearing on others is simply misguided.

Physicist Fritjof Capra has said, "There are solutions to the major problems of our time, some of them even simple. But they require a radical shift in our perceptions, our thinking, our values. And, indeed, we are now at the beginning of such a fundamental change of worldview in science and society, a change of paradigms as radical as the Copernican revolution."[2] There can be little doubt that we are living at the precipice of such revolutionary change. Some describe this change as the postmodern turn, others as the end of Christendom, others as the birth of globalization. Still others have linked these seismic shifts, suggesting that taken together they form something of a "perfect storm" for generating a paradigm shift in our vision of life.

I will not spend a great deal of time unpacking these mammoth shifts, as many resources do this well;[3] rather our concern lies with our perception, our hermeneutic, the lenses through which we see, interpret, and live. I hope to offer practical tools for seeing connections more clearly. I also hope to explore the theological and practical implications for church life, leadership, and mission. Together we will explore a networked kingdom lens.

> We have rather lost sight of the idea that Christianity is supposed to be an interpretation of the universe.[4]
>
> Dorothy L. Sayers

Paradigm Shift

The other day I was in a conversation with a couple who had recently gotten engaged to be married. Prior to their meeting, Mattie had thrown herself into the work of liberating women and children from slavery and the sex trade, while Tom's passions led him to focus on missional church planting. Individually, both Mattie and Tom had studied, dreamed, and accomplished much within their respective areas of calling, and each had a pretty clear sense of their life's direction. However, when they got engaged new questions emerged. Would they pour their joint energies into the much needed work of advocacy for voiceless women and children? Would they plant a missional faith community? Would they each do their own thing, or would they imagine some way of living into both passions?

Paradigm shifts start with a view of the world that is more or less coherent but still has a few vital unanswered questions. When some of those "vital unanswered questions" begin to find resolution, those new resolutions have a way of realigning much of what was known and believed previously. Prior to their engagement, one of the vital questions still unresolved for Mattie and Tom was, "Will I marry? And if so, to whom?" After resolving that question for each other, their life paradigm shifted. No longer could either of them chart the course of their life without considering the other. Their new paradigm invites them to navigate a shared vision of life.

Thomas Kuhn's book *The Structure of Scientific Revolutions* has served as the touchstone for thoughtful reflection regarding paradigm shifts. Writing with the scientific community in mind, Kuhn defines a paradigm as "the entire constellation of beliefs, values, techniques, and so on shared by the members of a given community and used by that community to define legitimate problems and solutions."[5] A paradigm is a view of life that is more or less coherent and agreed upon, so when a "paradigm shift" occurs, there is a revolutionary break with the accepted and generally unquestioned norms. Such revolutionary breaks with the accepted norms usually make it impossible to return to the previous paradigm of life. "I once was blind, but now I see"—that's a paradigm shift!

Many of the serious challenges facing our families, communities, and churches stem from the breakdown of the precritical assumptions, beliefs, values, and practices that together formed the "old" paradigm through which the modern world perceived life. The old paradigm that has dominated Western culture and church culture for the last few hundred years consists of a number of entrenched ideas, among which are the autonomy of the individual; the voluntary nature of community; a mechanical view of creation; life in society as a competitive struggle for existence; and belief in the inherent goodness of progress achieved through economic and technical development, to name just a few.

A caveat is due here; we would be wise to confess our tendency to label these paradigms as either "good" or "bad" (even the terms "old"

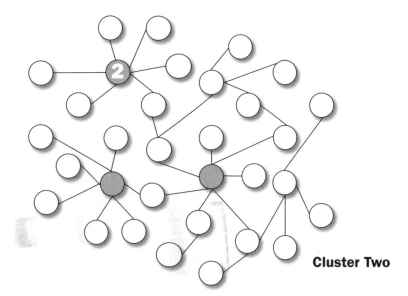

God's Networked Kingdom

The breakthrough theories behind Facebook, MySpace, and the social networking revolution will be explored in this cluster of chapters. Scale-free networks enable us to reimagine the kingdom of God in terms of being relationally connected with God, one another, and with all of creation.

After a general overview of God's networked kingdom, we will allow this relational paradigm to reshape our perceptions of both interpersonal relationships and the networked person.

The Networked Kingdom

Harnessing the Power of Social Networks

> To see connections, we must see connectively. That is, we see con-
> nections in and by making them. . . . Thinking relationally about
> relatedness embroiders new designs into the tapestry of relation.[1]
>
> Catherine Keller

As a bivocational church planter and pastor, I was always looking
for employment that was lucrative and had flexible hours, a difficult combination to find for someone with a seminary education.
During the first wave of the dot-com craze, I thought I'd found the
perfect position.

Having recently moved to the Seattle area, I'd been actively trying to pick up on the vibe of the city. My wife and I were out on
the town five to six nights of the week soaking in the culture(s) of
our new home, a missional form of cultural exegesis. We spent our
evenings at coffee shops, night clubs, art shows, concerts, and poetry
open mics, and had made a practice of visiting one or two churches
a week; in fact, we visited more than fifty churches in our first year.
Whenever possible we'd strike up conversations with some of the

people we bumped into, and occasionally we'd end up setting up a time for a longer conversation over a "triple tall middle of the road cappuccino."

Following up on a visit to a fairly new church in Issaquah over our beverages of choice, Chris, the pastor, asked me how I hoped to pay my bills given that the vision of ministry that I'd outlined for him seemed to have questionable financial viability. As I expressed my plan for intentional bivocational ministry, Chris told me that a friend of his named Woody was starting a new company and might be able to put me to work. Since at the time dot-coms were "going public" left and right, regularly transforming new crops of computer nerds into twenty-something millionaires, I figured this might be my opportunity to find that lucrative/flexible job that had eluded me up to that point.

I called up Chris's friend. Woody agreed to meet with me to see if I might be a fit for this new company. After a twenty-minute interview and overview of the company, I was hired. It was a business-to-business company that was first-to-market in a potentially lucrative volume software licensing world. The problem was the new company had very few customers. That's where I came in. It was now my job to find new clients. At the end of the interview, Woody started stacking telephone books on a folding table that was serving as a desk and told me I could start right then. He took the first phone book off the stack, opened it up to "IT Professions," and handed me a phone. And for the next three years, we grew our client base from a handful to over forty thousand clients. Little did I know that this job would radically alter not only my understanding of computer networks and social networks, but would open my eyes to the ubiquitous reality of all manner of networks while simultaneously transforming my paradigms of the kingdom of God, the church, and the relational patterns of life.

It's Not What You Know, but Who You Know

I visited the Issaquah church because I met a church denominational leader in Portland who thought Chris would be an important leader for me to know. After visiting his church and getting to know Chris, he linked me up with Woody. In turn Woody gave me an opportunity to experience networking in a different way than I had up to that point. I'm guessing we've all had similar experiences: meeting someone who in turn introduces us to someone else, who then connects us to someone or something we needed, forming a chain of connections that give life.

Though we'll talk more about this in subsequent chapters, this common experience is often referred to as Small World Theory.[2] It is the theory behind the Will Smith film *Six Degrees of Separation*, as well as the online game from a few years back called the "Oracle of Bacon," in which a person would try to find the connections between any celebrity and the actor Kevin Bacon. The theory demonstrates that every person is linked to every other person on the globe by about six "degrees" (in this case, people) of separation. So by connecting with a friend, of a friend, of a friend, of a friend, of a friend, you can connect with anyone, anywhere. Interestingly, I've since learned that most people find employment through a friend of a friend. People rarely recommend their closest friends for jobs; typically people feel more comfortable recommending friends of friends, the way I was hired by Woody. I was three degrees of separation away from landing my job at the high-tech firm.

As I began to learn about computer networks, and began to grow our client base through asking our clients whom they knew who might also be interested in the kinds of services we were providing, I began to see the connections between that work and my calling as a church planter.

Calzones, Conversations, and Connections

One afternoon I was out for calzones with a good friend who was part of our new church. He began to tell me about an article he had read in a recent issue of the *Scientific American*. The article, written by physicist Dr. Albert-László Barabási, was about the surprising new findings that Barabási and his team of Notre Dame researchers stumbled across as they sought to create a detailed map of the World Wide Web. What arrested my thinking was Peter's words, "Dwight, this article describes exactly what we're trying to do with our church plant." I was hooked.

Peter and I quickly finished our calzones and walked (almost ran) back to his place so I could see the article. I couldn't believe what I was reading. In just a few short paragraphs, Barabási walks through a brief history of the three-hundred-year-old study of network theory and paints a picture of how their new findings were changing everything that we thought we knew about how networks function. Their new network mapping provided tools to actually see how everything in creation is linked to everything else. They called this theory Scale Free Networking. Barabási begins his article by stating:

> Networks are everywhere. The brain is a network of nerve cells connected by axons, and cells themselves are networks of molecules connected by biochemical reactions. Societies, too, are networks of people linked by friendships, familiar relationships, and professional ties. On a larger scale, food webs and ecosystems can be represented as networks of species. And networks pervade technology: the Internet, power grids, and transportation systems are but a few examples. Even the language we are using to convey these thoughts to you is a network, made up of words connected by syntactic relationships.[3]

My imagination was ignited. Since that article was printed, there has been nothing short of an explosion in thinking, research, and application of these new Scale Free Network findings. Facebook, Twitter, LinkedIn, and an ever-growing number of other social networking applications are rooted in these recent discoveries and help us to see more relationally. And for anyone who longs for the kingdom of God to be more and more realized, then a vision of a networked kingdom is for you.

is present where he himself is present. Jesus described it as a place where captives find freedom, where those who can't see find new vision, where those who are stuck find movement again, where those without power are empowered, where the weak find strength, where the strong humble themselves in service, where those who feel lost are found, and where, when the lost are found, celebration erupts.[7]

> We are caught in an inescapable network of mutuality, tied in a single garment of destiny. Whatever affects one directly, affects all indirectly.[8]
>
> Martin Luther King Jr.

The Yeasty Expansion of God's Kingdom

One time when Jesus was asked what the kingdom of God is like, he described it using the process of yeast being worked through bread. As microbiologist Louis Pasteur demonstrated in 1857, introducing yeast into dough is not simply a mechanical, or even a chemical, process; it is a process of infusing life. Yeasts are a growth form of eukaryotic microorganisms classified in the fungi kingdom; basically, yeasts are living organisms that, by virtue of their life, naturally seek to grow and multiply. It is interesting to note that yeast is important as a model organism in modern cell biology research, and is one of the most thoroughly researched living networks. Researchers have used yeast to gather information about the biology of the eukaryotic cell and, ultimately, human biology. The image on the next page is a network map of yeast, showing the relation of proteins (the circles) and their interactions (the connecting lines). The fermentation process of yeast being worked through bread dough is a small but clear example of the sort of dynamic relationships that transform reality.

The other day as my wife and I were making pizza dough, it was striking to witness the dough expand as we created an atmosphere that allowed the yeast to do its "relational magic." After mixing the yeast in with the dough and placing it in a warm, dark place, the fermentation process was allowed to kick into full gear. Before long the dough was filled with little pockets of air, making for light,

A proteome sampler of 1,458 yeast proteins (circles) and their 1,948 interactions (lines)[9]

fluffy pizza crust. I'm not suggesting that Jesus was in some way foreshadowing Pasteur's work when he described the kingdom of God as being like yeast being worked through dough; rather, Jesus is describing the kingdom of God as a living reality that is present and active, though not always visible to the naked eye.

Jesus's parable highlights a few traits of yeast that are important for us. First, only a little bit of yeast is necessary to leaven a large amount of dough; that is good news for our world. Second, one cannot isolate the work of the yeast from the dough; they must be together with the appropriate environmental conditions. Finally, the living work of the yeast is nearly impossible to see with the naked eye. As Craig Keener says in his commentary on Matthew, this parable "most clearly declares that God's kingdom had arrived in some sense in Jesus's ministry, in a hidden and anticipated way. . . . Jesus's kingdom invades the world in a hidden way."[10] This hiddenness may be best understood in relational terms. Interpersonal relational connections are rarely flashy events or big programs; rather, they are the relatively mundane stuff of life—connecting with your neighbor and bringing them a casserole when a grandmother passes away, or building a friendship with the older man whose cubicle is next to yours. Simply connecting while living in the way of Christ is how the kingdom of God transforms the world. Though we'll talk more about this in future chapters, this parable suggests a very subtle but important understanding of life and the gospel. Life is a dance of chaos and order.

Near the school where I teach is one of the Pacific Northwest's great bakeries. Walking into Macrina's, one's nose is immediately filled with the scent of fresh baking, and there is always a fantastic array of breads to select from—from plain white and multigrain to far more exotic breads. In my rather selective memory as a child growing up in the Canadian prairies as a Mennonite, I thought there were only two kinds of bread: store-bought sliced bread and home-made bread. I still remember my first encounter with sourdough bread. It was during lunch while our family was laid over in the San Francisco airport. I have to admit it took me a while to warm up to its taste. But with my new awareness I walked into one of those little airport shops and saw sourdough starter kits for sale. Apparently, if a person purchased one of those starter kits and cared well for it, that starter kit could last your entire lifetime. Yeast can keep growing and spreading.

To limit this groundbreaking understanding of God's networked kingdom to the church would be like limiting yeast to a single loaf of bread. I don't think any of us can afford a "loaf theology," not when God has revealed Godself as the bread of the world. Yeast, like God's dream for creation, is the gift that keeps on giving. So throughout this book we will be exploring a connective vision of kingdom life. This, no doubt, will have a deep impact on churches, but it is first and foremost about connective life as God imagined it in creation, through the incarnation of God in Jesus Christ, and that will one day be fully realized.

Networks 101

For most of the three hundred years that networks have been studied, networks were thought to be random. "Random networks" have randomly placed nodes (dots, representing things, places, or people in relationship) with a relatively even number of links connecting the nodes to each other. A road map is a good example of a random network: it shows the cities and towns and the roads that link them together. On this map of Washington State, it doesn't matter if you're looking at Seattle or Walla Walla (bottom right corner); all the nodes (cities) have a fairly even distribution of links (highways). Contrast that with the flight maps we see in the back of in-flight magazines. Those network maps reveal instantly that Seattle has significantly more links connecting it to cities all over the world. This is a scale-free network map. Seattle is a "supernode"; it is a hub of flights. If a resident of Walla Walla wants to get to Hong Kong, they will need to get to Seattle first—one degree of separation.

WASHINGTON

When Dr. Barabási and his team first set out to map the World Wide Web, they assumed they would likely find an elaborate form of a random network with relatively even distribution of links between sites. But of course we now know they found something radically different. They found that some Web pages are radically more connected than other sites. Put simply, the nodes of a scale-free network aren't randomly or evenly connected. Scale-free networks include many highly connected nodes, hubs of connectivity that shape the way the network operates. The ratio of highly connected nodes to the number of nodes in the rest of the network remains constant as the network changes in size. So while a handful of sites may link to dwightfriesen .com, millions more are linked to and through the Amazon.coms and Google.coms of the Web world. There is not an even distribution of links; there are Walla Walla-type nodes, like my website, and then there are Seattle-like hubs. This makes the world much smaller, for by connecting to Google, the world of links open up to you.

This emerging field of study is not simply an abstraction for computer geeks and physicists but is already helping people in a vast array of fields to see more clearly how things are related to each other. It helped us better understand the spread of AIDs, how terrorist cells function and multiply, and how yeast permeates bread dough. For our purposes it holds tremendous possibilities for the people of God to reimagine (even reimage) the interrelationships of the individual person, the local church, and the kingdom of God.

In a comprehensive network map of God's scale-free kingdom, nodes would represent every aspect of creation, while links would illustrate their relationships. A comprehensive map like this would include the past, present, and future. In such a network map, nodes would not just include the living humans with whom we regularly interact but would also include saints of old, families of origin, geographical shapers, political influences, books, ideas, movements, organizations, weather patterns, mountain ranges, automobiles, roads, blogs, all manner of events, and so on. All shaping forces must be understood to be present within such a map; the complexity of such a map is truly unfathomable. So for the sake of simplicity here, we will primarily use nodes to represent human beings in our spheres of influence.

Like yeast, networks are living dynamic systems, with much activity and constant change. New nodes enter while others leave; new links develop while other links diminish in influence. Networks are so dynamic that any printout of a network map will be obsolete almost as soon as the ink is dry. God's networked kingdom is never static. The kingdom we experience today is different than the one experienced by Jesus two thousand years ago. It is still God who reigns relationally over *all*; but the *all* does not remain the same.

> Eventually, everything we currently believe will be revised. What we believe, then, is necessarily untrue. We can only believe in things that are not truth . . . I think.[11]
>
> Max Guyll, clinical psychologist

In this brief introduction of God's networked kingdom, we have been emphasizing the shifts in perception from atomized individuals to interconnected relational networks. In future chapters we'll further unpack the theological and practical implications of this networked kingdom vision of connective life.

Be ready for some surprises.

New paradigms have a way of reconfiguring what we thought we knew. We will see new ways of engaging theological questions and framing them within this relational paradigm.

> And precisely because from all eternity God's being is a being in becoming, God is already "ours in advance."[12]
>
> Eberhard Jüngel

Recommended Resources for Further Reflection

Albert-László Barabási, *Linked: The New Science of Networks* (Cambridge, MA: Perseus Publishing, 2002).

Mark Buchanan, *Small World: Uncovering Nature's Hidden Networks* (New York: Weidenfeld & Nicolson, 2002).

Fritjof Capra, *The Hidden Connections: Integrating the Biological, Cognitive, and Social Dimensions of Life into a Science of Sustainability* (New York: Doubleday, 2002).

Bob Ekblad, *A New Christian Manifesto: Pledging Allegiance to the Kingdom of God* (Louisville: Westminster John Knox Press, 2008).

Questions for Personal Reflection or Small Group Conversation

- Why is it that we are so drawn to the kind of spontaneous network of care that erupted at Ground Zero? How can our faith communities steward our presence, resources, and connections to encourage such spontaneous outpouring of love?
- What cautions or concerns are stirring in you as you consider a networked vision of the kingdom of God? What theological and ethical questions must we hold if we are going to wisely learn from the theories behind Facebook?
- Read Luke 13. What do you read in Jesus's two illustrations of God's kingdom?

2

Links

Different Kinds of Relationships and Why They Matter

An individual has not started living until he can rise above the nar-
row confines of his individualistic concerns to the broader concerns
of all humanity.[1]

Martin Luther King Jr.

If there was an "architectural endangered species list," then active
lighthouses would likely be near the top. Of course, many lighthouses can still be found dotted along the world's rocky shores;
they are symbols of the past, popular as romantic backdrops for
photographs, but of little functional use. Lighthouses are relics of
a time before sonar, radio, radar, and satellite navigational systems.
We know that lighthouses were once cutting-edge technology. In fact,
one of the seven wonders of the ancient world was the Lighthouse
of Alexandria, constructed on the island of Pharos in Egypt in the
third century BC. For centuries Alexandria's lighthouse was one of
the world's tallest buildings, standing roughly 450 feet tall. Yester-
day's technological advances are obsolesced by today's, and today's
technological advances will likely be obsolesced by tomorrow's.

Lighthouse of Alexandria

When sea travel was the only option for the world traveler and lighthouses were in their heyday, they were a welcome sight. Imagine being at sea for weeks and suddenly you spot a light on the horizon. During that era the "lighthouse" became a popular metaphor for followers of Christ. The lighthouse stood as a symbol for exploration and all things new. The lighthouse also stood as a symbol for individualism; the rugged lone person enduring the hardships of weather, standing against the elements for the sake of others; a bright light in an otherwise dark and dangerous sea; me against the world. In 1913 Walter J. Mathams penned the hymn "Stand Fast for Christ Thy Savior," in which the second stanza picked up on the lighthouse metaphor:

Stand Fast for Christ Thy Savior!

Stand faithful to the last!
Strong founded like a lighthouse,
That stands the storm and shock,
So be thy soul as if it shared
The granite of the rock.
Then far beyond the breakers
Let thy calm light be cast.

A modern, individualistic reading of Jesus's words in Matthew 5 often undergirds the use of the lighthouse metaphor. "You are the light of the world," said Jesus. "A city on a hill cannot be hidden" (Matt. 5:14 NIV). Shane Hipps rightly points out that our English translations of this important teaching of Christ can often cause us to miss the corporate nature of what Jesus was saying. "When Jesus uses *you* in '*You* are the light of the world,' it is actually a plural form of the word, meaning 'you all' or 'you, yourselves' (or if you're from the American South, 'y'all'). The word *light* in the Greek is strikingly singular." Hipps goes on to say that "we are not a thousand points of light; we are a corporate city on a hill."[2]

From a distance both lighthouses and cities signal their presence by emanating light, but that's where the similarities end. With a lighthouse, what you see is pretty much what you get; a standalone structure that sends off light as a warning signal of danger. But a city is different. Cities, while also sending off light, do not do so intentionally; most cites don't set "being a light" as a goal (though Paris and Las Vegas may). For most cities, being a light just happens. Simply by being a city, it is a light unto the world.

Cities are hubs of linking activity. They are complex living networks of people, buildings, roadways, utilities, and the like. Cities are interconnecting layers of related networks functioning together with the common goal of sustainable life for all. Cities are particular to their geography, history, economics, industry, and so on. They are dynamic. Cities are in a constant state of becoming. People are moving to and from cities, new homes are being built while older buildings are being demolished, new roads and airports are being added, new businesses are started while others close.

The layered networks of a city are so dynamic that when we begin to see with connective lenses we actually come to see that the lighthouse is in fact an extension of the city. The lighthouse is not really a standalone beacon as thought in the modern era but exists because of and for the sake of the larger network, serving as an emissary inviting sailors back to civilization. In this way individual persons exist in the context of larger social networks, and we do not want to lose sight of this tension. Networks provide context and relational meaning to individuals.

Theoretical physicist Fritjof Capra contrasts lighthouse and cities this way: "The basic tension is between the parts and the whole. The emphasis on the parts has been called mechanistic, reductionist, or atomistic; the emphasis on the whole, holistic, organismic, or ecological."[3] In the modern era we tended to see and study things in isolation; we dissected frogs, organizations, personal narratives, or even theologies in an effort to understand them, with the hope that by taking the thing apart, we would come to understand what made it work. Today we increasingly see limitations of that kind of divisive study. We now try to study things in their context to see how they relate in and with their environment. In addition to dissecting the frog, we realize we can learn a lot from studying the frog's habitat, how that habitat fits into an ecosystem, and how that frog's ecosystem is interrelated to our own.

Some thinkers have begun to refer to this as the "relational turn." Rupert Sheldrake, the British biologist and author of *A New Science of Life*, describes his own movement from lighthouse thinking to city thinking this way: "I chose biology because I loved animals . . . but I soon realized that the kind of biology I learned involved killing everything and cutting it up. Ever since, I've been driven by the question, 'What would it take to develop a science that enhances life?'"[4] Sheldrake's question is a *connective* question. His question marked his paradigm shift toward seeing relationally. Together we're asking a similar question: What would it take to develop a theological vision that enhances life?

Although a lighthouse can be a great place to retreat, to get away to have some alone time, it is not a great metaphor for imagining life in God's networked kingdom. A better metaphor for faithfully imagining following Christ is the *city*. Walking in the way of Christ is inherently relational. To follow Christ is to link up with God through the power and presence of the Holy Spirit, and to link up with the ever-becoming people of God, the city on the hill. It's all about linking. As leaders of churches and organizations, we are interested in relationships, both one-on-one relationships and the clusters of relationship that form a communal identity. What is an interpersonal relationship? What is your theology of relationship? And how do we understand the dynamic of interpersonal relationships clustering together in the formation of communal identity?

> Learning to observe the whole system is difficult. Our traditional analytic skills can't help us. Analysis narrows our field of awareness and actually prevents us from seeing the total system.[5]
>
> Margaret J. Wheatley

What Is a "Link"?

Links are relationships; it's that simple. So when we're looking at a network map, the line connecting any two nodes is a link. It's a visual demonstration of the relational connection between persons or things.

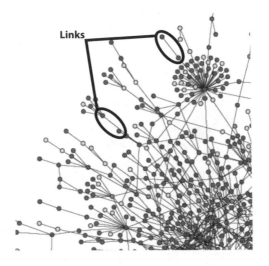

Most of the time when we think about interpersonal relations, we jump to specific "relationships" we have, often bringing to mind the people in our lives—our friends, family, co-workers, congregants, etc. We may bring those we love or those we love to hate to mind, but rarely do we consider the nature of relationship itself.

At a basic level, to have a relationship is to have a connection to something other than oneself.[6] We will begin by looking at two types of interpersonal relationships, drawing from the Austrian-Israeli-Jewish philosopher Martin Buber. Buber was among the first thinkers to propose a theory of interpersonal relationships. He proposed two primary types of relationships that every person needs for human flourishing. First we'll consider "*I & It*" relationships before moving to "*I & You*" relationships. Then we'll explore how the clustering of relationships form a shared communal identity, a "*We*" like the city metaphor we just discussed. One of the central themes of Buber's groundbreaking book *I and Thou* is that human life finds its meaningfulness in relationships, and all of our relationships bring us eventually into relationship with God, who is the "Eternal Thou."

I & It

When we relate with an inanimate object like a mug, it's obvious the link is an "*I & It*" relationship. The relationship is not reciprocal; you and the mug simply can't connect the way you can with another person or with God.

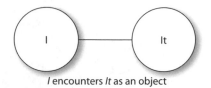

I encounters *It* as an object

However, we can also have *I & It* relationships with people. In an *I & It* relationship people do not actually meet even though they may be face-to-face. Rather than a genuine encounter, the *I* sees the other person as an idea, or a conceptualization, and treats that person as an object. An obvious example might be when a person views pornography; they see an image of a person but the person is lost to them. The viewer fails to encounter the hopes, dreams, and story of the other person, and thereby misses their shared humanity. They reduce the "other" to little more than a thing for *I*'s own gratification. Most "*It'ing*" is more subtle. Consider marriage. If I begin to conceptualize Lynette as "wife," I objectify her with my notion of a "wife." I end up missing the fact that she is a glorious person created in the image of God; I pigeonhole her into my vision of a role. Even though part of her identity is linked to her "wifeliness," she is and always has been more than "wife." I'd be an utter fool not to open myself up to encountering Lynette in her fullness.

In the *I & It* relationship, an individual has the tendency to approach an encounter through a utilitarian lens, treating other things, people, or even God as an object to be used and experienced. In this way *I & It* relationships are safer—I can control the encounter. *I & It* relationships reinforce that all others exist for *I* and to be used by *I*; and this is important for functioning in society as we need to be able to relate with others based on our perceptions of others' roles or functions in our given networks.

I sometimes wonder whether part of the allure of websites like Facebook and MySpace is that they promise an *I & You* encounter for the low price of an *I & It* relationship. All a person has to do to become your "friend" is send a quick request and then wait for your confirmation. And since I get to control my home page, displaying only the images and content I want the world to see, conversation is not necessary nor is a hug or a meal or anything even remotely humanizing in terms of the analog world. Having said this, I also know the depth of connection I have experienced online, especially through chat applications such as Skype, but I do want to think critically and theologically about what these technologies promise and what they can deliver.

Before you beat yourself up for *It'ing* a relationship, it is impossible for people to have genuine *I & You* encounters with everyone all of the time. For instance, imagine what would happen if a person who works in retail tried to have *I & You* encounters with every person they encountered in a day. They might lose their mind and most certainly lose their job. I want to be crystal clear that *I & It* relationships are not bad; in fact, they are necessary for healthy living. Just as every person is unique, so is every relationship. People matter to God and relationships matter to God. Just as you wouldn't want or expect every person to be the same, we can expect the same kind of variety in our linking.

In a networked city we encounter people all the time whom we relate to as *It's* by the function they play in the larger network. When you order your latte, you relate with the barista as a coffee merchant; when you go to your child's school, you relate with your child's teacher as an educator. Just imagine how it might work to open yourself up to an *I & You* encounter the next time a telemarketer interrupts dinner. Buber argued that human life is something of a dance between *I & You* and *I & It*; in fact, genuine *I & You* experiences are rather few and far between. But those moments of genuine encounter are moments we treasure, they are the stuff of poetry and art, and the possibility of such linking is a strong motivator for me to get out of bed each morning.

51

I & You

The second way of relating Martin Buber draws our attention to is the *I & You* relationship. *I & You* relationships stress the mutual, holistic existence of two persons linking together. It is a genuine (contrasted to "objectified") encounter, because these persons meet one another in their authentic existence, without any qualification or objectification of one another. Not even imagination and ideas play a role in this relation; we simply encounter each other person. An *I & You* relationship lacks any composition or structure and communicates no content or information; the two people connect as the wholeness of one person encounters the wholeness of another.

If you're like me, then you have had moments when you are with someone—maybe someone you've known for a long time, or even someone you've just met—and something almost mysterious happens. It's as though the two of you connect—you feel heard and seen and known. That's the *I & You* encounter.

Of course you can't prove that kind of connection and you can't really explain it; it is just something that happens, and it is always a moment of grace and truth. Despite the fact that *I & You* cannot be proven or measured, it is real and perceivable. Buber even emphasized that this is the only way in which it is possible to interact with God, and that an *I & You* relationship with anything or anyone connects in some way with the living God. This is not to diminish in any way God's self-revelation in Christ and through Scripture; rather it highlights the illuminating presence of the Holy Spirit. Many people experience an *I & You* encounter with God in their conversion, first communion, a baptism of the Holy Spirit, centering prayer, or other disciplines, but most often the *I & You* experience with God is felt in the encounter with another human being. To experience this *I & You* relationship with God, a person must be open to the idea of such a relationship, but not actively pursue it. The pursuit of such a relationship tends to create qualities associated with it, thereby preventing an *I & You* connection, limiting it to *I & It*.

Centuries before Buber, the Christian mystic Meister Eckhart said something similar: "I pray to God to be rid of God." By this Eckhart meant that he wanted to be so present to the possibility of genuine encounter with God in God's fullness that he opened himself to surrender all his prior thoughts, experiences, and theologies that might reduce God to an idea or a conceptualization. Buber says by being open to the *I & You*, God will eventually come to you.

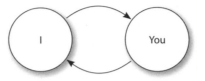

Our understanding of links within God's networked kingdom becomes even more exciting when we consider the incarnation of God in Jesus Christ. In Christ we see God open Godself up to the possibility of genuine encounter with human beings. Theologian James Cone suggests that God's *I & You* movement toward genuine encounter with human beings is indicative of the existence of an *I & You* relationship between God and humanity rather than an *I & It*. This means that God does not just reveal Godself through a narrative but presents Godself to us in a person to be encountered. God confronts the human person in Jesus Christ as *You*—as a person—not as *It*. Our status before God as *You* rather than *It* confers a *You*-structure on creation in its totality. Because of God's *I & You* movement toward creation, human beings are able to relate to one another as *I*'s and *You*'s just as God, in Jesus Christ, relates to creation as *You*. So we rightly speak of "having a personal relationship with God" precisely because God-in-Christ, by the power of the Holy Spirit, opens Godself up to the possibility of genuine encounter with you; it has been the very dream of God since before the creation of the universe.

Realizing that we've just covered some pretty complex ground, I want us to pause and reflect on some of the links that make up our own little nodal clusters in God's networked kingdom. Who are some of the people with whom you've enjoyed genuine encounter? How has your life been shaped by such encounters? Or, who are some people you relate with primarily through their roles or functions? How might your vision of interconnection be transformed by opening yourself up to a genuine encounter with someone you've seen primarily in their role(s)? How does God's movement in Christ toward genuine encounter with humanity give you hope for how you might move toward others? Reflecting on such questions opens us up to the wonder of reconciliation.

Becoming an open "We"

Buber provides a useful framework for understanding the relationship of two nodes in a network map. Now we turn our attention to the shared identity that comes from multiple nodes linking together to form a "*We*." Our faith communities are not simply one-on-one relational encounters; there is also a shared sense of *We*. And this *We* identity is not an exclusionary "us versus them," but is a differentiated *We* for the blessing of all. The apostle Peter speaks to the formation of the early churches' new shared identity:

> Come to Christ, who is the living cornerstone of God's temple. He was rejected by the people, but he is precious to God who chose him. And now God is building you, as living stones, into his spiritual temple. What's more, you are God's holy priests, who offer the spiritual sacrifices that please him because of Jesus Christ. As the Scriptures express it, "I am placing a stone in Jerusalem, chosen cornerstone, and anyone who believes in him will never be disappointed." Yes, he is very precious to you who believe. But for those who reject him, "The stone that was rejected by the builders has now become the cornerstone." And the Scriptures also say, "He is the stone that makes people stumble, the rock that will make them fall." They stumble because they do not listen to God's word or obey it, and so they meet the fate that has been planned for them. But you are not like that, for you are a chosen people. You are a kingdom of priests, God's holy nation, his very own possession. This is so you can show others the goodness of God, for he called you out of the darkness into his wonderful light. Once you were not a people; now you are the people of God. Once you received none of God's mercy; now you have received his mercy. (1 Peter 2:4–10)

"Once you were not a people but now you are." God's mission is more than the salvation of individuals; it is also the formation of a people who participate with God in the reconciliation of all and the re-creation of the world. This is the already-present and yet-to-be reality of God's networked kingdom. *We'ing* is the big picture that mobilizes and gives purpose and shared identity to every church, and every person seeking to walk in the Way of Jesus.

Jesus's "high priestly prayer" of John 17 is a *We'ing* prayer. In three movements he talks with his Father about their relationship; then about his cluster of disciples; and then in his final prayer movement, he prays for us. He prays that *we* would be one, just as he and the Father are one, that just as the Father is in Christ and Christ is in the Father, that *we* will be one in them. God opens up God's own being to make room for *us*. Andrei Rublev, one of the great medieval iconographers, wrote[7] an icon of the Trinity sitting around a table with an open space at the table for us. In the incarnation of God in Jesus Christ, a place is set for creation at God's table.

Andrei Rublev, "The Trinity"

We refer to it as an "open *We*" because the people of God are not a hermetically sealed group of elect holy men and women who stand apart from culture or society. Rather, our new networked identity as a people is to be a blessing to others, like yeast worked through dough, like a cluster of blessing in the complexity of a city. As we proactively seek to help life flourish while also proactively standing against injustice and the oppression of life, we embody the "open *We*" of God.

This vision of a networked kingdom does not come out of some new technology of network mapping, nor does it even come from God's creative imagination; rather, it's born of the being of God.

The Linking God

The Christian understanding of a linking God is surely one of the most unique claims of any religion or system of thought in the world. Many religions believe in one God, or multiple gods, or even no god; but only Christianity has a vision of a God who exists in relationship even before time—a God whose "being," as Orthodox theologian John Zizioulas says, is "in communion"; a God who moves relationally toward creation, not away from it; a God who is personally and actively involved in human affairs, not just setting things in motion. And we don't stop there; we believe that God created all that is out of love and for relationship, and we understand the very mission of God, as seen throughout the capacious narrative of revealed Scripture, to be the reconciliation of all things relationally unto God. This is a God who cares about links. This is a God who has not shown Godself to be a "standalone lighthouse"; rather God has revealed Godself as a dynamic city, diversity in oneness. And the church has understood this diversity in oneness as "Triune." Although the metaphor of the city cannot hope to capture the fullness of the mystery of the Holy Trinity, it does help to underscore the dynamic of God's oneness and God's plurality.

At the end of the seventh and beginning of the eighth century, John of Damascus, a Syrian monk and priest, used at term that has helped many people appreciate the wonder and beauty of God's complex being of diversity in oneness. John of Damascus was a renaissance man of sorts; he was deeply interested and contributed to the study of law, theology, philosophy, and music, and he was the chief administrator to the ruler of Damascus. In his effort to describe God's dynamic inner relational life as seen through the narrative of Scripture, he used the word *perichoresis*.[8] The word combines two Greek terms that, loosely translated, paints a picture of the persons of the Trinity living the

of God and others. The networked person values human agency, freeing the person to pursue justice and act prophetically within his or her community. The networked person also values her or his God-givenness while not collapsing into fatalism, for they take seriously the personal and moral responsibility to be cocreators with God in the earth's re-creation.

As we saw in the first chapter, social networks are social structures made of nodes (generally individuals) that are linked together with others, forming a complex web of relations. What is so exciting about this kind of network mapping is that as we visually demonstrate our self-identity, we recognize that we cannot understand ourselves without the larger web of others who give language, story, and shape to our existence. Within a map of a social network, I see that I exist and am in community with God and others.

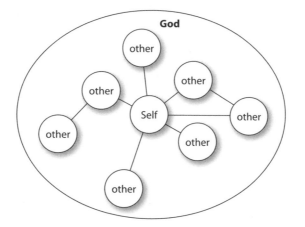

We've already begun to appreciate some of the ways that network theory is helping us see all that is with fresh eyes. Emerging technologies are equipping us like never before to map complex realities. Network theory is proving to be of great value as we seek to faithfully understand ourselves in community. While we can be tempted to define ourselves with the easy poles of individualism or social construction, a robust vision of a networked person can redeem both definitions by holding them in a dynamic tension enlivened by the presence of the Holy Spirit. Both individualism and socially constructed understandings have shortcomings and profound gifts. But recent technological advances are actually confirming what trinitarian Christians have always understood, even if our language has been different in different eras.

The capacious narrative of Scripture reveals that God creates human beings in God's own image. Often those words roll off the tongue with such ease that we forget that the God in whose image we are created is triune. God is multiplicity and oneness—three persons, one God. This great divine mystery is vital to understanding the networked person. For you are a unique human being—no other person has your narrative history, your unique passions and gifts. And you are part of a much larger story, one that begins even before the creation of the universe(s); you are part of the human story, united with all of creation by our shared Creator. And what we're discovering and beginning to understand more fully today than at any other time in recorded history is that who you are, how you live, and what you do impacts every other living being and living system on the earth.

This is why it has never been more important to develop a functional understanding of the networked person. Failure to live into your networked identity can have (and has had) disastrous results. Without owning our interconnectedness to all that is living, we trade God's Edenic mandate to humanity for thinking only of ourselves and our "kin," without regard for the family of humanity. Without living into God's dream for the connective kingdom, we will perpetuate false dichotomies—either/or, us versus them, the haves and the have nots. But thanks be to God that reconciliation is possible.

Many pastors, scholars, social activists, business leaders, and even politicians are daringly inviting us to live into the very interconnections for which we are created. Consider what just a few of them are saying:

- "Whatever affects one directly, affects all indirectly. I can never be what I ought to be until you are what you ought to be. This is the interrelated structure of reality."[3]—Martin Luther King Jr.
- "The life I touch for good or ill will touch another life, and that in turn another, until who knows where the trembling

stops or in what far place my touch will be felt."[4]—Frederick Buechner

- "We have a stake in one another . . . what binds us together is greater than what drives us apart, and . . . if enough people believe in the truth of that proposition and act on it, then we might not solve every problem, but we can get something meaningful done for the people with whom we share this Earth."[5]—Barack Obama

- "The kind of thinking we need about ourselves and our place on the planet—our interrelationship and interdependence with all other human beings and other life-forms—has been deadened by the hand of a consumerist/militarist paradigm that exalts the comfort and superiority of elite individual human beings . . . a communitarian view of human beings is an ecological, economic one. It is a view of our place in the scheme of things that sees our well-being as interdependent with all other life-forms in a just, sustainable way. . . . God's household is whole planet; it is composed of human beings living in interdependent relations with all other life-forms and earth processes."[6]—Sallie McFague

- "Systems thinking is a discipline for seeing wholes. It is a framework for seeing interrelationships rather than things, for seeing patterns of change rather than static 'snapshots.' It is a set of general principles—distilled over the course of the twentieth century, spanning fields as diverse as the physical and social sciences, engineering, and management. . . . During the last thirty years, these tools have been applied to understand a wide range of corporate, urban, regional, economic, political, ecological, and even psychological systems. And systems thinking is a sensibility—for the subtle interconnectedness that gives living systems their unique character."[7]—Peter Senge

- "The reality today is that we are all interdependent and have to coexist on this small planet. Therefore, the only sensible and intelligent way of resolving differences and clashes of interests, whether between individuals or nations, is through dialogue."[8]—the Dalai Lama

- "All things are connected like the blood that unites us; we did not weave the web of life. We are merely a strand in it. Whatever we do to the web, we do to ourselves."[9]—Chief Seattle
- "Our interconnectedness on the planet is the dominating truth of the twenty-first century. One stark result is that the world's poor live, and especially die, with the awareness that the United States is doing little to mobilize the weapons of mass salvation that could offer them survival, dignity and eventually the escape from poverty."[10]—Jeffrey Sachs
- "When one tugs at a single thing in nature, he finds it attached to the rest of the world."[11]—John Muir
- "*Independence* . . . middle-class blasphemy. We are all dependent on one another, every soul of us on earth."[12]—George Bernard Shaw

This is just a small sampling of the growing multitude of voices inviting you and me to live connectively as we open our eyes to the world of connections while taking responsibility for our interconnectedness.

So what? How might embracing the networked self serve us and all of humanity?

Humbly Holding Your Understanding of "Self"

Make no mistake about it; holding the mystery of human identity to be a networked identity is very challenging, for the human tendency has been to claim greater certainty of identity and self-mastery than such mystery will allow. As Walter Truett Anderson has written, "All human societies are built upon a lie, the lie of self-conceit that we know what a human being is and can satisfactorily describe one with the customary names, roles, and badges that are the currency of all our lives."[13] Part of living into a networked understanding of the self involves living with greater humility. You are both more and less important than you ever imagined. And most often we see ourselves dimly though as through a dark glass (1 Cor. 13:12).

Needing "The Other"

Even a cursory glance around most of our homes reveals an obvious needfulness of others. Most of us don't grow all of our food, design and sew our clothing, or cut down trees to make our own furniture, let alone manage the systems providing our water, electricity, and trash removal.

Seattle was hit with a significant ice and snowstorm a couple of years ago. Our home was without electricity for three days, though some areas of the city were out much longer. When the power first went out, it was kind of a novelty, maybe even a little fun. We lit candles, made a fire, roasted hot dogs, and camped out on the floor in the living room. But after three days of trying to stay warm while trying to keep everything in the freezer from melting, the novelty had worn off. While we were struggling to read by candlelight, we knew that utility crews were working 24/7 to restore power. These tangible, real-world goods and services are worth celebrating and fostering thanksgiving for, and we can receive them as the gifts that they are. Often we are reminded of our needfulness of others when tragedy strikes or we are brought face-to-face with our own limitations.

There is another kind of needfulness of others that is even more difficult to live into. How are you needful of the panhandling home-less veteran you pass as you walk from your bus stop to your place of work? How are you needful of the displaced Sudanese refugee who is wondering when or if they can return to their village? How are you needful of the tattooed inmate whose name and story you will likely never know? You get the idea. If we truly are interconnected, then the existence of every person, whether we will ever benefit personally from them or not, contributes to the complex fabric of the human experience.

That last sentence contains a problematic phrase, especially for those of us in the Western world: "benefit personally." In our com-modified context, we readily see the value of disciplining ourselves to be grateful for those whose lives and work directly benefit us, but for those whose lives don't directly benefit, we can all too easily write them off, ignore them, or see them as a problem.

In a detailed network map, nodes are interconnected. Though we may be separated by "six degrees of separation" in some cases, whatever happens to one happens within our shared network, and we feel the impact indirectly. Though you may not feel the immediate impact that the fifth-grade Iraqi boy felt when his school was bombed, through just a few degrees of separation, your summer vacation plans have now had to be changed due to rising fuel prices. We are all connected.

Maybe the most important reason to embrace our need of those who don't benefit us in obvious ways has to do with God's vision of mission for the connective kingdom. As we begin to understand our interconnectedness, we begin to take on a shared mission: the mission of kingdom connecters is to actively participate in the blessing of others. To say it another way, the mission of life in God's networked kingdom is to participate in the ending of suffering of all kinds. Kingdom connecters know that when one person suffers, we all suffer, and that to bless one has untold ripple effects.

Embracing the Gift of Conflict and Difference

Active participation in the ending of suffering and in the blessing of others applies to everyone. It applies to those whose lives directly benefit us and those we will never meet. It also applies to our enemies. A networked person embraces conflict with the faith that hidden inside every conflict is an opportunity for the reconciling gospel to be made visible; the greater the conflict, the greater the opportunity for the gospel to be manifest. If reconciliation is the gospel in action, then every time a networked person encounters an "enemy," they see an opportunity for grace to transform a relationship. In God's networked kingdom, reconciliation is the eschatological hope embedded within enmity.

The networked person embraces their need for others, including their enemies. A networked person can actually embrace the fact that conflict is an iron-sharpening-iron gift. Relationships with other people who differ in profound ways provide a unique opportunity for the networked person to reflect, forgive, repent, or differentiate in hope of encountering the other. In many ways, the transformational process of being formed in the image of God as seen in Jesus Christ by the Holy Spirit happens best when we have the privilege

70

of being in relationship with those who differ from us or even those who consider us their enemies. I am not suggesting in any way that a networked person will be able to resolve all conflicts—this is not some utopian vision—rather the networked person is able to imagine the needfulness even of those who disagree with them in profound ways.

Offering a Differentiated Self

That last statement may have you scratching your head. How is the transformational process served by being in relationship with those who disagree with me or even think of me as their enemy? Again, this is where the networked paradigm helps us see that the strength of a network is not a network of sameness. Network vitality is rooted in needful difference. Think of the food chain network. No, I'm not talking about McDonald's and Taco Bell. I mean the feeding relationships between species within an ecosystem. In order for the entire ecosystem to thrive, each species plays a vital role. In the simple diagram here, if we were to eliminate the snake, the ecosystem would be flooded with grasshoppers, while the hawk would lose its food supply.

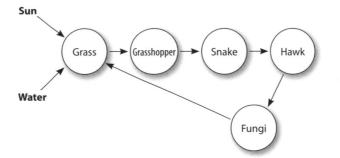

From a networked kingdom perspective, the snakes of our lives are a gift. Now, I'm not suggesting that we need more enemies, nor am I suggesting that we should devour those who disagree with us. Rather, I want to stress that our lives are enriched—that is, we grow and are most healthy—when we hold our most difficult relationships

71

with an eye on the much larger context in which we experience those conflicts.

I am part of Emergent Village, which is an organization that is part of the much larger emerging church conversation. In the last few years, as the emerging church conversation has been invigorating both the evangelical movement and mainline traditions, spurring innovative church planting and stimulating missional communities committed to embodying the gospel all over the world, Emergent Village has come under scrutiny. Coming under scrutiny is rarely enjoyable. I know I often feel defensive initially, but when I realign my perspective along the lines of God's networked kingdom, I come to a healthier conclusion. The networked paradigm enables me to better appreciate that those challenging the values and actions of this conversation are vital to the health of the ecosystem of faith. As those with different perspectives, concerns, narratives, communities, and theologies offer the fullness of themselves in relationship, and not just critique, the whole community of faith is served.

Rediscover God's Call to Participate in Blessing Others

People of the Book have come to treasure the first few paragraphs of the twelfth chapter of Genesis as the call of Abram. In these few sentences God and Abram enter a relational covenant of blessing. God promises to bless Abram and his children and to make Abram's family a blessing to others.

> Then the LORD told Abram, "Leave your country, your relatives, and your father's house, and go to the land that I will show you. I will cause you to become the father of a great nation. I will bless you and make you famous, and I will make you a blessing to others. I will bless those who bless you and curse those who curse you. All the families of the earth will be blessed through you."
>
> So Abram departed as the LORD had instructed him, and Lot went with him. Abram was seventy-five years old when he left Haran. He took his wife, Sarai, his nephew Lot, and all his wealth—his livestock and all the people who had joined his household at Haran—and finally arrived in Canaan.

Traveling through Canaan, they came to a place near Shechem and set up camp beside the oak at Moreh. At that time, the area was inhabited by Canaanites. Then the LORD appeared to Abram and said, "I am going to give this land to your offspring." And Abram built an altar there to commemorate the LORD's visit. After that, Abram traveled southward and set up camp in the hill country between Bethel on the west and Ai on the east. There he built an altar and worshiped the LORD. Then Abram traveled south by stages toward the Negev. (Gen. 12:1–9)

This is not the first divine invitation to be a blessing or to live in such a way that other lives are blessed. The first invitation to be a blessing is seen within God as God elects to bless in and through creation. Within the creation narrative is God's first invitation to humans to live as a blessing; this invitation comes in the Garden of Eden when God entrusts the stewardship of creation to humanity. Stewarding creation is about living with resources in a sustainable way that blesses others so all have access to the provision of God. Nor is Abram's call the last time we see God call followers to live as a blessing. For throughout the Tanakh and the New Testament, the prophets and apostles consistently seek to reorient God's people around the service and blessing of others. Often this is expressed in participating in the end of suffering, whether it is caring for those whom the rest of society has forgotten (the widows, orphans, and strangers), touching the lepers (the AIDS victims of Christ's day), or helping those who worship an unknown God discover the hope, meaning, and salvation of the God made known in Jesus Christ. Suffering takes many forms and therefore blessing takes many forms. Just this week, my neighbor told us that she is being tested for cancer, I learned that a dear friend and his wife are filing for divorce, and a friend's eleven-year-old son lost his battle with leukemia. And that's just one week. The invitation of God, as seen most profoundly in incarnation and the life of Christ, is to enter into suffering as a blessing: not to condemn the world but to save it. Surely, this is part of what Jesus means when he summarizes all the teachings of the Law and the Prophets as love of God and love of neighbor (Luke 10:27).

The networked person lives with the reality that we are all interconnected, and that hidden in the midst of all the stuff of life is an opportunity to bless others. The networked person wonders "What if?" What if I blessed rather than cursed? What if I sought reconciliation rather than division? What if I oriented my life around serving more than hoarding? The networked person imagines and acts on our already present connection in and through our shared humanity and in the Spirit of our Creator. Sounds a little like the prayer of St. Francis:

Lord, Make Me an Instrument of Your Peace

Where there is hatred, let me sow love;
where there is injury, pardon;
where there is doubt, faith;
where there is despair, hope;
where there is darkness, light;
and where there is sadness, joy.
O Divine Master, grant that I may not so much seek
to be consoled as to console;
to be understood as to understand;
to be loved as to love.
For it is in giving that we receive;
it is in pardoning that we are pardoned;
and it is in dying that we are born to eternal life. Amen.[14]

Recommended Resources for Further Reflection

Stanley J. Grenz, *The Social God and the Relational Self: A Trinitarian Theology of the* Imago Dei (Louisville: Westminister John Knox Press, 2001).

Paul Ricoeur, *Oneself as Another* (Chicago: University of Chicago Press, 1992).

Charles Taylor, *Sources of the Self: The Making of the Modern Identity* (Cambridge, MA: Harvard University Press, 1989).

Questions for Personal Reflection or Small Group Conversation

• Who are you? What stories do you tell when people ask about who you are? What do those stories reveal about yourself as a networked person?

- Why is embracing conflict so difficult? How does a person who has been seriously hurt or abused by another needful of even the perpetrator of the abuse?
- Review the list of quotes. What is stirred in you as you listen to what these men and women are calling us to rediscover?
- What do you find most hopeful about seeing yourself as a networked person? And how does it give meaning to you as an individual person?

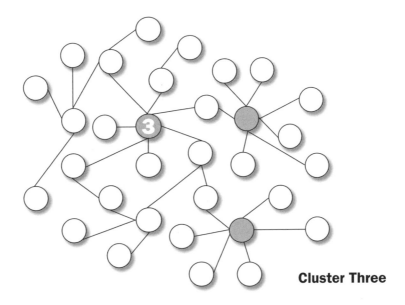

Cluster Three

Leading That Connects

This third cluster of chapters focuses on defining the role and responsibilities of leaders within the networked vision of God's connected kingdom, and articulates the necessary function of chaos for the sake of church health.

Connective Leaders

The Parable of Google

[Connective leaders] focus on common ground, the connections among people, not on the contrasts and chasms that separate them. Of course, connective leaders recognize the differences, but they welcome them as a source of multithreaded strength. By loosening the bonds of individualism, they use diversity to brace interdependence, to stimulate innovation, and to serve the needs of all. For these reasons, if for no other, connective leaders are our best hope for achieving renewal through interdependence.[1]

Jean Lipman-Blumen

While teaching an MDiv elective at Mars Hill Graduate School titled "The Kingdom of God and the New Sciences," I invited the learners to collaborate in the creation of a network map of our collective journeys to the school. Using the same whiteboard, the learners each drew nodes representing leaders, books, family members, websites, conferences, and friends with links, forming a visual topography of their relational journey to enrolling at this particular school to continue their missional training. The one thing I asked was that each node could only be created once; so once a node was on the board, the next person would simply create another link to that node, enabling us to see if any of the nodes were disproportionally connective in our collective network map. By the time the whole class had finished, we discovered a clear hubbing pattern, and it was not what I'd expected to find.

My hypothesis had been that the primary influencing hub (in network theory a "hub" is a node composed of an a unusually large number of links) would have been one of our core faculty, or our school's president, or maybe one of the school's numerous conferences or workshops. But much to our surprise we found two disproportionally connected nodes, and neither of them was a staff member or a conference.

One of the most connective hubbing nodes was www.mhgs.edu (the school's website), and the other was Brian McLaren. Now Brian used to serve on the school's board of directors, he worked very closely with us in the redesigning of our MDiv program, and he has taught at the school from time to time, but he is not and has never been a resident faculty member. Nonetheless, for the group of students in that room, he was a significant hub connecting them to their ongoing missional education. This ad hoc network map reinforced what I have already known of Brian: he is a connective leader. Numerous times I've received phone calls or emails, or have met someone at a conference, and our conversation begins with, "Brian recommended we connect."

A couple of chapters ago we contrasted two metaphors of the Christian life, the "lighthouse" and the "city." Connective leadership is "city leadership," marked by a relentless passion for openly sharing its resources, links, knowledge, and relationships when an opportunity for collaboration or reconciliation emerges. Connective leadership is about active participation in the lives of those within one's community so as to link people with those things contributing to the flourishing of lives.

By contrast the standalone lighthouse practice of leading tends to control its use of knowledge and resources, most often sharing such resources only when it directly serves lighthouse purposes. For those functioning within the lighthouse paradigm, knowledge is power and power is best kept to oneself. In keeping knowledge, relationships, and links to resources close to itself, lighthouse leadership tends to create a culture of dependency around the leader.

This chapter will unpack connective leadership by exploring the simple question, "Who is a leader in God's connected kingdom?" The next chapter will explore in greater detail how a connective leader functions. And though we're looking at the definition and the function in separate chapters, they are inseparably linked. For "who a leader is" is inextricably connected to what a leader does—a reality that we all know and will be reinforced in multiple ways in the coming pages.

The Parable of Google

Google.com is helping me understand connective leaders. Rarely does anyone visit Google.com for the sake of Google itself; rather we connect with Google when we are searching for something or someone, maybe an answer to a question that's plaguing us, or even a better question. . . . Basically, we go to Google because we've come to trust that Google will consistently link us to what we seek. Google is a hub, not of information but of *links to* information; its entire goal is to provide the very best links to the seeking person. Google is a matchmaker that connects the seeker with the best options being sought. This networked vision of leadership is vital to understanding who a connective leader is and what relational authority is in a networked vision of the world. What I am calling, "The parable of Google" can equip us in thinking more biblically about the nature and function of Christian leadership in churches, organizations, businesses, and families.

Connective Authority

Google's linking "authority" is not derived from a position or a title and has no intrinsic authority; instead its authority is earned through consistently serving its users by giving away the very connections it has. Google has no authority in our lives other than the authority we freely give it. The more effectively Google links us today with what we seek, the more we trust it to be a faithful hub tomorrow. Google's present authority is rooted as much in our past experience of its faithful linking as it is to the quality of the links it provides, and it is with that history of effective connecting in mind that we will return to Google the next time we need to perform a Web search. Google's authority is located in the consistent achievement of its mission to provide links to the best sources on the Web. The present authority given to Google, which is rooted in our past experience, has a future orientation that goes beyond Google. This future orientation is rooted in the person seeking connection for the sake of lived life. In this way there is an eschatological hope for a preferred future in and through the connections we seek.

Having said this, Google cannot assume our followership. Google's commitment to helping people find the most meaningful links propels the people behind Google to be always growing, learning, changing, and getting to know those they serve so that the links offered will most likely serve those who are seeking. Just recently Google added "promote" and "remove" features into their search engine to improve the links it provides. But if Google were to deviate from its connective mission and cease to provide the best links, you and I would quickly find another search engine that could better serve the hubbing role necessary for life . . . maybe Microsoft's Bing.

I don't know how this parable of hubbing leadership connects with you, or how it sparks your kingdom imagination. As for me, I find myself increasingly curious about the kinds of links people seek through their connection with me. How can I live as a Google-like linker of meaning-making connections and suffering-eliminating relationships? How can I retrain my eyes to see and my ears to hear the kingdom possibilities that are already and always present each time my life intersects with another? The parable of Google reminds me that those in my life are never simply connected to me for the sake of me, but that I also connect the people in my life to that which is beyond me. In fact I have an ethical responsibility to those I'm connected with to help them thrive; toward that end I find myself prayerfully seeking to become an ever-more connective person so that I may be faithful in serving those with whom I'm connected. I also recognize that the connections I have been blessed with are not my possession but are a gift to steward with wisdom, humility, and openness.

Consider my relationship with my son. We love each other, yet his connection with me is never an end in itself; he is connected with me in part so that one day he can "leave" me and live into his unique life and calling. As a father I am always striving to empty myself of the best links, resources, relationship, and narratives I have that will help my son live life to its fullest.

Kenotic Matchmakers

I was only two years old when *The Fiddler on the Roof* was released in movie theaters, but even now I can sing along for at least a couple of lines when the milkman's daughters start singing, "Matchmaker, matchmaker, make me a match." Although the matchmakers of yesteryear may have fallen on hard times, through the rise of Web-based social networking platforms, online dating services are thriving. Twenty-first century matchmakers such as eHarmony and Match.com, and the scores of similar services for the corporate world such as Monster.com and CareerBuilder.com, highlight one of the vital functions of connective leaders: connective leaders help people make wise connections.

For those people summoned to serve as connective leaders within God's networked kingdom, relationships are everything—relationships with God, relationships with one another, and relationships with creation. Nodes cluster around hubs not just for the personality or charisma of the connective leader, but also for the uniquely embroidered relational mosaic that is the connective leader. When a person connects to a connective leader, a whole new world of possible links open up to other nodes through that leader—other people, ideas, institutions, attitudes, resources, etc.[2] So while Max DePree has challenged us to "understand that relationships count more than structure,"[3] which is very true, the connective leader also understands that relationships *are* the deeper structure.

A connective leader offers their best links, their best relationships, and the best of themselves to others. The apostle Paul describes Christ's self-emptying connectivity this way:

Your attitude should be the same as that of Christ Jesus: Who, being in the very nature of God, did not consider equality with God something to be grasped, but made himself nothing, taking the very nature of a servant, being made in human likeness. And being found in

83

appearance as a man, he humbled himself and became obedient to death—even death on a cross! (Phil. 2:5–8 NIV)

The above passage from the apostle Paul's letter to the church in Philippi is often referred to as the *kenosis* passage. *Kenosis* is the Greek word for self-emptying. *Kenosis* is the idea of holding nothing back in the movement of offering life to another. Thomas F. Torrance defines *kenosis* this way:

> The love of God revealed in Jesus Christ is his total unconditional self-giving to mankind, love in which he does not withhold himself from loving to the utmost or cut short its full movement, and it is upon that love that our hope of redemption and resurrection is grounded. It is the love of the eternally self-affirming and self-giving God, and so the love he pours out freely upon us through the Holy Spirit is love that affirms itself as love against all that is not love or resists his love. . . . He does not hold back his love from the sinner, for he cannot cease to be the God who loves and loves unreservedly and unconditionally.[4]

That's what connective leaders do; they humbly serve those connected to them, linking them to others even at great personal cost. The incarnation, life, and death of Jesus Christ is the ultimate act of connective leadership. It is an act of humble self-emptying service to which Christ is summoned by his community, the Triune God in relationship with creation. Christ's love for the other two persons of the Godhead, and his love for humanity and all creation, compel him

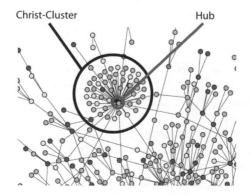

Christ-Cluster   Hub

to serve as a hub. His connective action on the cross is self-emptying for the sake of relationship. Christ, the connected, relationally bridges God with humanity in the ultimate act of redemption and reconciliation while simultaneously bridging human to human.[5]

Relational bridges, or links, flow both ways. Both the hub and the node are influenced by their mutual relationship. People responding to an invitation to serve as a connective leader seek out opportunities to be influenced by others. They do this because the health of a Christ-Cluster requires multiple links—even weak links—that bridge outside one's immediate cluster. The multiplicity of links bridging beyond an immediate community is what knits the members of a local church into the larger fabric of God's connective kingdom. When faith communities live into the links beyond their immediate community, they find a type of intrinsic accountability stemming from the infinitely larger network.[6] This gives meaning and definition to the local church. This bridging beyond itself is a like cross-pollination. Without connections beyond itself, the rogue faith community could assume a type of totalitarian, heretical, cultish tone, or any manner of other idiosyncrasies, further reinforcing its isolation from the rest of the network.[7] This bridging beyond itself also opens up new missional opportunities for bearing witness to God's reconciling work. We'll explore implications for this in an upcoming chapter.

Any thoughtful person serving as a connective leader for a faith community will seek to link its participants with other nodes within their cluster, but they will not stop there. Connective leaders will aid each connecting node in weaving a web that safely and uniquely cradles that node. As David Bjork writes,

> They understand the need to integrate the converts into the Christian community, which they see as a networking of mentoring and accountability relationships which are distinguishable from ecclesiastical structures and which transcend denominational distinctives.[8]

Who Is a Connective Leader?

Who is a connective leader? Well, from a networking perspective, all relationally linked nodes will naturally influence each other.[9] As J. Oswald Sanders writes in his modern classic *Spiritual Leadership*,

"leadership is influence, the ability of one person to influence others."[10] In this way every person is a leader. In the networked kingdom of God it doesn't matter if you are the CEO of a Fortune 500 corporation, a stay-at-home mother of two, a junior high girl who loves to blog, or the priest of a two hundred-fifty-member suburban Catholic church; you are a leader. The question is not "Are you a leader?" but the relative scale of your influence.

If we take another look at a network map, we see that every node is connected to other nodes, but some nodes are disproportionately well connected; these super connected nodes are called hubs. A word of caution here: from a "lighthouse" perspective, a person could think that in a networked vision of the world the goal would be to pursue the creation of links so as to bolster one's own influence. This can and does happen. We've all seen people "work" a room for personal gain, like the Amway salesperson who manipulates their network of friends as a means of widening their base of clients. Such network manipulation is a gross distortion of the power of relationship, for it reduces relationship to the level of personal gain. The goal of connective leadership is not to gain more links to increase the scale of your own influence, but to help those connected to you make meaningful connections that will help them find fullness of life.

Connective leaders live relationally with those in their communities. Connective leaders are not born; they are summoned into being.[11] It is our relationships and the people with whom we're linked that call forth our leadership. All calling forth to leadership service is occasional, contextual, and reflective of the people with whom we're doing life. To put it another way, leaders are not summoned in such a way that they remain leaders indefinitely. Alistair McFayden, who writes profoundly on the call to personhood in community, describes this connective leadership dynamic this way: "We are called into being as persons by the expectations others have of us. These are framed and mediated to us through their form of address—the way in which they intended us in their communication."[12] As the ethos of your affective community morphs, so does its ethos invitation for connective leadership.

Part of the reason why a connective vision of God's kingdom is such an exciting concept is that it helps us to see afresh that the connective leader does not stand apart from those he or she is leading; the leader is an active participant within their small network of connections, being formed, reformed, and transformed by the community(ies) and culture(s) in which their influence is summoned; it is a dynamic process. It is important to note that this vision of connective Christian leadership is rooted in a deep belief that the Holy Spirit is an ever-present, active person shaping and calling forth kingdom of God connections, inviting and empowering us toward God's dream for all creation.

The "Leader" Label

I have to confess I have a deep struggle with the word "leader"; the idea of leadership has all too often been misused to push agendas, lord over, and control. We often do ourselves and our churches a disservice when labeling people as "leaders." We create a false dichotomy between leader and follower. This false dichotomy can all too easily lend itself to abuse by the person socially labeled as "leader" while encouraging a type of disengagement from person(s) socially labeled as "followers." Peter Senge of MIT challenges our fixed understandings of leadership:

> Our traditional views of leaders—as special people who set the direction, make the key decisions, and energize the troops—are deeply rooted in an individualistic and nonsystemic worldview. . . . At the heart, the traditional view of leadership is based on people's powerlessness, their lack of personal vision and inability to master the forces of change, deficits which can be remedied only by a few great leaders.[13]

As we are exploring connective leadership within a framework of God's networked kingdom, we must look first at God, in whose social image humanity is created. The apostle Paul encouraged the young church in Corinth to look at Christ when they wanted to understand God. When Paul wrote, "Christ, who is the exact likeness of God" (2 Cor. 4:4), he was saying that to see Christ is to see God. And what we see of God in Christ by the Holy Spirit is not always what we would expect.

87

We see the Lord Jesus Christ baptized by John despite the Baptizer's protests that it ought to be the other way around. We see Jesus ask a lot of questions and, by contrast, give few clear answers.[14] We see Christ challenging the religious establishment as much as, if not more than, the Roman occupation. We see a Christ who is at times lonely and scared. We see Christ scandalously engage with the outcasts and powerless in Jewish society, such as women, Gentiles, lepers, Jewish sellouts to the Romans, and unlearned people. When opportunities seem to present themselves for Jesus's fame to increase, he often asks people to keep things hush-hush. Early on in his teaching career, he has large crowds eating out of the palm of his hand; by the end of his life just a handful of close friends are left, and even they scatter when it gets tough, not to mention that one of his closest associates sells him out. In death he is nailed to a Gentile cross on Jerusalem's garbage heap to die alongside common criminals. And we best not forget that he was born out of wedlock, in a stable, and placed in a feed trough by a teenage girl who claimed to be a virgin.

"Christ, who is the exact likeness of God." God reveals Godself to be the kind of leader whose power is in powerlessness.[15] God is the true connective leader whose influence comes not from title or position but from being in relationship within Godself, missionally moving toward all creation in a spirit of reconciliation and re-creation. A God who cares not for the power of God but joyfully empties such divine rights and privileges to connect and reconnect with those God loved and led. And this emptying is not just some kind of humble gesture; it is in fact essential to what it means for God to be love.

I hope it's becoming clearer in your heart and mind that this biblical vision of a relationally connective kingdom holds the key to a profound sense of hope and possibility for you and me and the communities in which we live; for it reorients our vision of life, relationship, and ministry from the perspective of the Triune God who creates us in God's own relational image. And it transforms the dominant leadership imagination of the world, calling forth another way—a gospel way—of being in the world. It sparks one's imagination for incarnationally presencing oneself in the places of disruption within one's own network. You can be a reconciling presence, knowing that you are not there to "fix" others but to open your heart to mutual transformation through relationship.

Recommended Resources for Further Reflection

Dan B. Allender, *Leading with a Limp: Take Full Advantage of Your Most Powerful Weakness* (Colorado Springs: WaterBrook Press, 2008).

Douglas Griffin, *The Emergence of Leadership: Linking Self-Organization and Ethics* (London: Routledge, 2002).

Jean Lipman-Blumen, *Connective Leadership: Managing in a Changing World* (New York: Oxford University Press, 2000).

Questions for Personal Reflection or Small Group Conversation

- Think back on some of the connective leaders in your life; how did they offer themselves to you and how did they help you connect to those things you most needed?
- What did the parable of Google spark in your kingdom imagination?
- In what ways are other people finding meaning making connections through you? How might you be even more intentional in this connective service?

5

Leading Connectively

How Chaordic Life Reorients Leading

Relationships are not just interesting; to many physicists, they are all there is to reality.[1]

Margaret J. Wheatley

This chapter is about one simple and transforming possibility born of God's networked kingdom. It's about connective leaders leading connectively. It's about reorienting the things we do, the roles we play, the services we provide, and the links we offer around the *missio Dei*—the mission of God. Of course how we understand *missio Dei* will shape everything we are and everything we do. The mission of God is life.

The Hebrew Bible, the New Testament, and the life of Jesus Christ relentlessly and passionately demonstrate God's mission unto life. "Life" at first glance may sound far too simple to be the mission of God, but not when we stop and consider God's revealed narrative. God is true life, the great "I Am." God creates life as we understand and experience it. God sustains life. Everything that lives and breathes does so because of God. God redeems life, resurrects unto new life.

God's justice and judgment also point toward the kind of life that is God's dream for creation. When Jesus gave voice to his mission, he said, "My purpose is to give life in all its fullness" (John 10:10). As connective leaders, it is vital that we reorient all that we do around God's vision for fullness of life.

It's in the Gospel of John where we read Jesus's missional words about fullness of life. As the Johannine community compiled and edited the Gospel of John under the inspiration of the Holy Spirit, they knit a number of "I am . . ." stories and sayings of Jesus together, giving us as strong sense of the life-giving, connective identity of the mission of Jesus.

- "I am the Messiah!" (John 4:26);
- "I am here! Don't be afraid" (John 6:20);
- "I am the bread of life" (John 6:48);
- "I am the light of the world" (John 8:12);
- "I am not alone—I have with me the Father who sent me" (John 8:16);
- "I am the gate for the sheep" (John 10:7);
- "I am the resurrection and the life" (John 11:25);
- "I am going to prepare a place for you" (John 14:2);
- "I am the way, the truth, and the life" (John 14:6);
- "I am leaving you with a gift—peace of mind and heart" (John 14:27);
- "I am the true vine" (John 15:1);
- "I am sending them into the world" (John 17:18).

One such "I am" story tells of Jesus's encounter with a blind man. Jesus's disciples were curious about why the blind man had been born without sight. "Was it a result of his own sins or those of his parents?" (John 9:3, paraphrase mine). After responding to the disciples' inquiry in typical Jesus fashion, the story takes a public turn. The neighbors of the formerly blind man were divided about whether he was in fact the same blind man they had known since his blind childhood; some said "Yes," while others said, "No, but he sure looks like him."

The neighbors end up taking their sight-restored friend to see the Pharisees. Here is where the story gets interesting. If restoring sight wasn't interesting enough, the man shares his story without trying to defend or form an apologetic for his newfound sight. He simply tells his story; I was blind . . . I met Christ . . . now I see. Sadly, the religious leaders did not joyously enter into celebration over their blind neighbor who could now miraculously see; rather they were concerned about who healed him, and the fact that he'd been healed on a Sabbath day of rest.

This story concludes with Jesus turning and speaking to the religious officials. "I have come to judge the world. I have come to give sight to the blind and to show those who think they see that they are blind" (John 9:39). Jesus's statement elicits a "You talkin' ta me?" from the Pharisees as they rightly pick up that Jesus was calling them on their own blindness.

Well, this story bridges to the next one. In the beginning of the next chapter, Jesus contrasts the Pharisee-like thieves who climb over the wall to steal sheep and the hired hands who run away at the first sign of trouble with the "good shepherd." "The thief's purpose is to steal and kill and destroy. My purpose is to give life in all its fullness. I am the good shepherd. The good shepherd lays down his life for the sheep" (John 10:10–11). Life! Jesus says that he came to give life and life in all of its fullness. Connective leading is all about orienting all that we are and do around the fullness of life as witnessed to throughout Scripture and the life of Jesus.

Giving life in all its fullness (or abundant life) is the very reason God physically entered the human story in Jesus Christ. God is the author, creator, sustainer, and redeemer of life. So it only makes sense that the living God, who is the God of the living, would missionally orient Godself around giving fullness of life.

If the previous chapter helped frame our understanding of what a connective leader is, then this chapter will focus on the functional orientation of connective leaders. What does leading connectively look like? The church by the power and presence of the Holy Spirit continues Christ's ministry in the world, and that would suggest that the church's mission is to partner with God in helping life to flourish for all. Other functions like preaching, evangelism, administration, stewardship, pastoral care, and the myriad of other connective leadership tasks are oriented in and through God's dream for abundant life for the whole of creation. Therefore to grasp the significance of leading connectively in God's networked kingdom, we need to take a closer look at Jesus's own mission statement. We need to look at what we mean when we say "fullness of life."

Although Christianity has become a religion, the way of Jesus is "metareligious." It is about life—complex, rich, dynamic, relational, abundant life. As Leon Morris writes, "There is nothing cramping or restricting about life for those who enter His fold."[2] The Father is the creator of life, Christ is the redeemer of life, and the Spirit is the very breath of life. The Triune God offers the fullness of life to creation and to all of humanity. This is God's mission: that human beings like you and me would live as fully alive, fully networked human beings.

Sounds pretty good, right? But what is life?

> Life is a process of becoming, a combination of states we have to go through. Where people fail is that they wish to elect a state and remain in it. This is a kind of death.[3]
>
> Anaïs Nin

What Is Life?

In 1944 Nobel laureate in physics Erwin Schrödinger set out to answer this question. Recognizing the vastness and interdisciplinary nature of the question he was seeking to address, Schrödinger began his now-famous book *What Is Life?* by describing his as the "Naïve Physicist's Approach" to the question of life.[4] It is only fitting that I adopt a similar stance, that of a naïve pastor/theologian. As a naïve pastor/theologian seeking to understand not only what biological life is, but also what the full life is that Jesus described as his mission, I have grown keenly aware of the immensity of this question. Yet, if flourishing life is God's idea and gift, it is worth trying to understand, if simply out of worshipful appreciation for the wonder of receiving it.

My son is eight years old. And sometimes it feels like every moment with him is pregnant with possibility. For every one of my answers, he has questions; for every plan I have, he sees an adventure that may not look like the plan I've envisioned. Into my relatively ordered existence, my son often brings both chaos and life, and I wouldn't want it any other way. After all, that kind of chaos is the wonder of relationship.

Before Pascal had learned to speak—like many young children these days—Lynette and I had taught him some basic sign language so he could communicate with us: signs for "bottle," "more," "pacifier," and "sleep." One night as our house church was coming to the end of a time of worshiping God in song, Pascal made the sign for "more." The community responded and we sang another song. As that song came to an end, he made the sign again, and so on. As a young toddler without the use of spoken language, Pascal ended up leading his church community in a life-giving time of worship, altering his pastor's (dad's) plans for the service.

Parenthetically, it's a wonderful thing to be part of a community of faith where everyone's presence and participation can shape a gathering like this did. Of course it's not just children who call forth life by bringing chaos and order into relationship (though children seem to have a unique flair for it)—I do it, you do it, they do it, and, as the bumper sticker says, "life happens." Glorious surprises and unforeseen tragedies have a way of bringing order and chaos into relationships, often changing the course of our existence. Fullness of life is not embracing the glorious while sidestepping the tragedies; rather fullness of life is saying yes to God's invitation to fullness in and through embracing the dance of both the tragedies and the glories.

As connective leaders you and I actually can orient what we do around holding tragedies and glories together. We can minister in such a way that unpredictability and order can coexist in God's mission of abundant life. In fact, that's how I'm defining life: *life is the relationship between chaos and order.* Explore your own experiences of life and see if these two allies don't find each other.

> There are as many nights as days, and the one is just as long as the other in the year's course. Even a happy life cannot be without a measure of darkness, and the word "happy" would lose its meaning if it were not balanced by sadness.[5]
>
> Carl G. Jung

95

Chaos and Order

Don't be alarmed by the claim that life is the relationship between chaos and order; after all, did the Spirit of God not hover over the primordial chaos and speak forth life? Or consider the two trees in the Garden of Eden; one was the Tree of Life and the second was the Tree of Knowledge of Good and Evil. The dance of chaos with order is fullness of life. The wise writer of Ecclesiastes seems to have this relationship in mind when he writes, "There is a time for everything, a season for every activity under heaven. A time to be born and a time to die. A time to plant and a time to harvest . . ." (Eccl. 3:1–8). A time for chaos and a time for order.

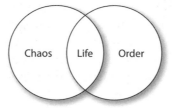

These two states are needful allies. Even more, God seems to delight in bringing about both chaos and order. "Chaos" is often used as a synonym for disorder, anarchy, or mayhem, but that isn't what the origin of the word suggests,[6] that isn't what chaos theory explores, nor is it how we will use the term. For our purposes we'll use "chaos" to mean "unpredictability." Chaos is not antiorder; in fact chaos theory has helped us to understand that there is an order to chaos; we call that order life. Often when one is able to step back and view the chaos in its larger context, what at first appears unpredictable reveals a pattern of order, as in the case of fractals.

A fractal, according to Benoît Mandelbrot, the Polish-French-Jewish-American mathematician and the father of fractal geometry, is "a rough or fragmented geometric shape that can be split into parts, each of which is (at least approximately) a reduced-size copy of the whole,"[7] a property called self-similarity. Because fractals appear similar at all levels of magnification, they are generally regarded to be infinitely complex. In creation we see many examples of fractals, from mountain ranges to the clouds that cover them, to bolts of lightning, coastlines, ferns, and snowflakes. Think of fractals as a mathematical metaphor for stepping back from chaotic unpredictability with the hope of discerning a pattern.

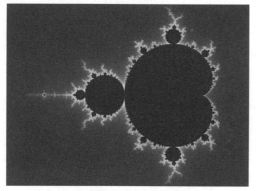

Fractal (Adriano Macchietto)

I wonder what might have happened if the Roman Catholic Church would have had a networked vision of God's kingdom when Martin Luther nailed his Ninety-five Theses to the Wittenberg church door? How might history have been different, how many lives might have been saved, if the Roman Church could have stepped back from the chaotic unpredictability with the hope of discerning a pattern calling forth newness of life?

Embracing life as the dance of chaos with order is an invitation to look for relational patterns in creation and community. This is remarkably hopeful because it suggests that when we encounter something that we couldn't have predicted, the very thing that we couldn't have predicted likely holds the key to a fresh move toward justice and reconciliation. The founder and former president of VISA famously coined the term "chaordic" to help those in his company imagine their organization harmoniously, allowing for the coexistence of chaos and order with neither behavior dominating.[8] If we are orienting our ministry leadership roles from an imagination shaped by God's connective kingdom, then the greater the disruption to our ordered existence, the greater the opportunity for the good news to be manifest.

It may be helpful for us to dip into chaos theory just for a moment to get a clearer vision of how the dance of chaos and order can produce life in surprising ways. Chaos theory is a subset of complexity studies that explores the causality or the relationship between events.

Chaos theory demonstrates that any seemingly insignificant event in the universe can potentially set off a chain reaction that will change the whole system. This is often referred to as the "Butterfly Effect." The Butterfly Effect demonstrates that in theory, the flapping of the wings of a butterfly might create tiny changes in the atmosphere that may ultimately alter the path of a tornado, or delay, accelerate, or even prevent the occurrence of a tornado in a certain location. If small and seemingly insignificant things can form the initial conditions for significant change, what might that suggest for reorienting our leadership to the flourishing of life?

A few years ago Mars Hill Graduate School sent me as a representative to a "Missional Church" conference in Washington, DC, sponsored by Off-the-Map. My friend Joe Myers was scheduled to present a workshop titled "Organic Church," so I was pleased to attend. At the last moment Joe was unable to proceed with his workshop. Joe made the recommendation to the Off-the-Map folks that I fill his workshop slot. I facilitated the workshop which a young church leader named Scott attended; Scott later picked up an application for Mars Hill Graduate School, and now he and I have the privilege of learning together. Now clearly this little chain of events is not nearly as dramatic as the "Butterfly" illustration, but it makes the point that you simply never know the full impact of what you say and do.

You can see why this is important for thinking about the church and human relations, for chaos theory describes the behavior of certain dynamic systems, that is, systems whose state evolves with time.[9] If human beings, our interpersonal relations, and creation are dynamic systems, then our local faith communities would be dynamic systems as well. This is why it is so important for us to reorient our kingdom imagination through a networked lens, for it helps us to see afresh the relational connections and the unimagined impact of a butterfly's flapping, attending a conference, nudging a friend toward life, protesting injustice . . . you just never know.

Chaos out of Order

In the creation story highlighted at the beginning of this chapter, God draws order out of chaos. Yet much of the rest of Scripture shows God bringing chaos (unpredictability) to a comparatively ordered existence. Think of God interrupting Abram's comfortable life by inviting him to leave for an unknown destination. Think of the Tower of Babel and introduction of linguistic diversity or the angel's announcement to Mary. Think of almost any of the Hebrew prophets whose challenging messages often called for or resulted in chaotic movement. Or think of Jesus, who claimed he did not come to bring peace to the earth but a sword (Matt. 10:34).

A proverb for life-giving connective leading might be, "In the face of chaos connective leaders participate in bringing order, and in the face of order connective leaders participate in the bringing of chaos." And yet we know that proverbs by definition are overstated truisms that point us in a helpful direction, but are best understood as hyperbolic. You and I both know that relationships and ministry are too complex for a proverb like that to serve us and our communities well in every situation. But more often than not, proverbs prove true. When a faith community only knows order without chaos, they can drift into faithless stasis. When a faith community only knows chaos without order, they will struggle to trust their participation in God's narrative. But when chaos and order dance together, dynamic faith rooted in God's story finds hope in the midst of a changing context. In our ordered communities, holy chaos can be embraced as a life stimulus; and in our communities of chaotic unpredictability, holy order can bring rest. And it is in this chaordic dance that we find life. From this emerging networked kingdom perspective of life, consider some of the ways chaos and order serve our communities of faith.

Get Smart: The Myth of Chaos versus Control

The premise of the 2008 film *Get Smart*, starring Steve Carell as Maxwell Smart/Agent 86, pits KAOS (the bad guys) against CONTROL (the good guys). This reinforces a number of modern myths that we still feel in our lives and ministries. One is that chaos (unpredictability) is a bad thing, which we've already discussed. The second is that the appropriate leadership response when confronted by the unpredictability of life is to try and exercise greater control.

Leading connectively in God's networked kingdom is not about controlling, but shaping the contour of your network through linking and resourcing unto fullness of life.

The idea of control is something of a myth. Who is in control? "Well I am. It says so right here in the church bulletin next to 'Senior Pastor.' That's my name." It's a natural, albeit misguided, assumption to equate being in control with one's positional function in any organization. But if you're not in control, who or what is? This is exactly the kind of question that this vision of God's networked kingdom enables us to reimagine; and what we need to reimagine is not simply the answer to that question but the question itself.

The control myth lies beneath much of the abuse and violence in our world, in our ministries, and in our families. It lies beneath much of the conflict in our faith communities, and lies beneath many distorted images of God. Margaret Wheatley makes this observation with respect to the control myth:

> Ever since uncertainty became our insistent twenty-first century companion, leadership strategies have taken a great leap backward to the familiar territory of command and control. . . . How is it that we failed to learn that whenever we try to impose control on people and situations, we only serve to make them more uncontrollable? All of life resists control. All of life reacts to any process that inhibits its freedom to create itself. When we deny life's need to create, life pushes back. We label it resistance and invent strategies to overcome it. But we would do far better if we changed the story and learned how to invoke the resident creativity of those in our organizations. We need to work with these insistent creative forces or they will be provoked to work against us.[10]

Leading connectively busts the myth of control and proactively dethrones hierarchies, daringly linking people and organizations with God's vision of the connective kingdom and surrendering their personal vision for ministry. In more hierarchal models of organizations, knowledge and connections were seen as power and the person with the most was in control. Knowledge and connections were therefore often held tightly by the leader. But leading connectively invites a redefinition of power. Power is very important in living networks, but it is not hoarded; it flows as a relational lubricant. The parable of Google and network theory more generally expose the control myth by helping us see that true power is in the giving of knowledge and connections to those seeking. As Sally Morgenthaler has said, "Leadership in a truly flattened world has no precedents. Never in the history of humankind have individuals and communities had the power to influence so much, so quickly. The rules of engagement have changed, and they have changed in the favor of those who leave the addictive world of hierarchy to function relationally, intuitively, systemically, and contextually."[11]

What might it look like for your faith community to begin thinking of itself as a resource center whose primary goal is to develop relationships with those people you're connected with? What might it look like to reorient your energies around connecting them with the very best resources at your disposal in order to help them thrive in their area(s) of passion?

While referencing Isaac Newton in a discussion of the role of collaboration in the evolution of living systems, Martin Nowak of the Program for Evolutionary Dynamics at Harvard University said, "If you were obsessed with friction, you would have never discovered this law."[12] If we are obsessed with control, we will never discover the wonder of participating in God's connected kingdom. Leading connectively dethrones the tool of hierarchy and busts the control myth. Connective leaders serve as hubs, linking people to the very best of their resources and relationships unto God's dream of fullness of life.

> Leadership is more tribal than scientific, more a weaving of relationship than an amassing of information.[13]
>
> Max DePree

Recommended Resources for Further Reflection

Tim Keel, *Intuitive Leadership: Embracing a Paradigm of Narrative, Metaphor, and Chaos* (Grand Rapids: Baker Books, 2007).

Sally Morgenthaler, "Leadership in a Flattened World: Grassroots Culture and the Demise of the CEO Model," in *An Emergent Manifesto of Hope*, ed. Doug Pagitt and Tony Jones (Grand Rapids: Baker Books, 2007).

Margaret J. Wheatley, *Leadership and the New Science: Discovering Order in a Chaotic World* (San Francisco: Berrett-Koehler, 2006).

Questions for Personal Reflection or Small Group Conversation

- Review Jesus's "I am . . ." statements from the beginning of the chapter; what do you observe about Jesus and his mission?
- If the mission of God is about the flourishing of life in the most holistic sense imaginable, how might your mission be reoriented?
- What did you find yourself saying as you read the depiction of life as the dance of order with chaos?
- Think of a time when you experienced a group that was not controlling but in which power flowed between people. What would have to happen for that spirit to transform our church and organizations?

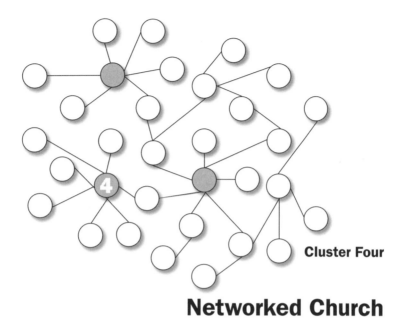

Cluster Four

Networked Church

This fourth cluster will drill into some ways a relational vision of God's networked kingdom can help us repurpose our understanding of the local church and its structures.

We will begin by looking at institutional churches, what we will be calling Christ-Commons. We will see that the primary function of the Christ-Commons is the creation and stewardship of a connective environment where missionally clustering in Christ is more likely to occur.

Next our focus will shift to the spontaneous and organic nature of Christ-Clusters, and how these dynamic living clusters missionally shape local and life-giving connections for their nodes, both animating and transforming institutional church structures.

Taken together these chapters enable us to imagine the unification of the "Body" and the "Soul" of local faith communities within God's networked kingdom.

Christ-Commons

Reimagining the Body of the Institutional Church

The basic problem with the new species of global institutions is that they have not yet become aware of themselves as living.[1]

Peter Senge

"What is the church?" If you're like me, you hear this question batted around from time to time. Because I'm able to spend much of my time with seminary students, I get to invest a fair bit of energy around the question. I decided to Google it. I jumped online and keyed in "define:church." I discovered that The Church is a rock band from Australia; an English surname; a film directed by Michele Soavi; a train station in downtown Buffalo; a song by hip-hop/R&B/rap artist T-Pain; and the list went on. Of course two more typical definitions also came up: "a place for public worship" and "one of the groups of Christians who have their own beliefs and forms of worship." It's these last two definitions that we will explore in the next two chapters.[2]

In these two chapters God's relational vision of the networked kingdom will dare us to reimagine both our institutional church structures and our more organic life as a people of God. Even though we will be considering these two aspects of church life in separate chapters, they are truly interdependent and interanimating. Our institutions and our organic social clustering are to the church what the body and soul are to the person: inseparably one.

Truth be told, we in Western church traditions have long struggled to maintain a unified vision of body and soul, often lapsing into thinking that the soul is good and the body is bad, and occasionally the other way around. Often we have a similar struggle with the church, thinking that the organic social and spiritual life of the church is good and the institutional structures of the church are bad. As a church planter I often found myself bemoaning the structural aspects, from money invested in buildings to business meetings, publishing newsletters, updating our website, or attending to denominational responsibilities. But I loved our relationships, our worship, and our service. Our age-old impulse to separate body from soul comes from an ancient belief called Gnosticism, which our early church leaders deemed a heresy. Gnosticism denigrates God's creation of human beings and leads to distorted understanding of the full humanity and full divinity of Christ. So we strive for a more unified vision, and as we are about to peer through the network lens of God's connective kingdom, we can rediscover the unity of the body and the soul of our churches, and in the process find fresh missional purpose for each.

The focus of this chapter will be on the institutional or structural understanding of church. In this chapter as in the next, I will be introducing new terms to describe either the body or soul of the church. We begin with the body: the church's institutional life. From the perspective of God's networked kingdom, these structures are best understood as "Christ-Commons." After propping up the contours of the term for definition, we will explore just a few of the ways the emerging vision of Christ-Commons missionally reimagines institutional structures. Reimagining church structures inevitably raises questions about the role of the pastor and the nature of authority, so we'll go there. But first, what do we mean by a "Christ-Commons"? I'm so glad you asked . . .

Christ-Commons

A "commons" is a connective space like a village square, a plaza, a forum, the Internet, or any open meeting place; I often picture Boston

Common (the oldest public park in the United States). Commons serve a variety of functions, chief of which is to provide a place for people to connect. But in Boston Common, since it is a park in which one might connect with nature, I can imagine many people heading out to the commons for some quiet time. If the commons is a village square, then merchants, vendors, and the village news might be some of the important connections. One of my other favorite commons is Seattle Art Museum's Sculpture Park. Since the Sculpture Park is just two blocks from my school, I often stroll through the park to reconnect before or after a class, or just to be outside enjoying the juxtaposition of God's creative works with humanity's creative works. Commons are connective spaces.

Our institutional church structures are also connective spaces. Of course this is nothing new; churches have always been open spaces to connect with God through Christ and by the Holy Spirit, while also creating a space for followers in the way of Jesus to connect with each other while serving the world. A Christ-Commons is a visible structure, institution, denomination, building, worship service, or small group that is formally created with the hope that the structure will provide an environment or space where people are more likely to experience life in connection with God and one another.[3] Christ-Commons exist primarily to provide elaborate systems of support that promote and equip people to cluster together in Christ's service as a blessing to others. Think of it as the dance of form and function. The form is the Christ-Commons and the function is the collaboration of the Holy Spirit with people clustering together in a particular time and space actively participating with God in reconciliation, justice, and blessing. If the structure or form of a Christ-Commons were to seek to exist for itself, it would be like a corpse: life would have left the body. And without a structure, there would only be a disembodied spirit of some kind. Body and soul are united and needful of one another. Our church structures create and steward connective spaces linking those gathering with God and each other while giving embodied expression to life lived in the way of Christ.

I wonder what the people in your faith community would say the primary purpose of the church is? Or what might the people in your neighborhood who don't participate (at least in any obvious ways) in your faith community say about the primary purpose of your church?

The great news is that your church is a connective space. What might it look like if your church focused even more intentionally on becoming a connective space? How might your community steward its structure(s) so as to create an even more fertile environment where meaningful connections with God, each other, the world, and creation would be more likely to form? Christ-Commons repurpose our institutional structures as places where kingdom of God connections are more likely to be made. God's dream for the flourishing of life as seen in Jesus blossoms when people form kingdom connections.

> The opposite of love is not hate, it's indifference.
> The opposite of art is not ugliness, it's indifference.
> The opposite of faith is not heresy, it's indifference.
> And the opposite of life is not death, it's indifference.[4]
>
> Elie Wiesel

Christ-Commons: Structural Life Support

As your faith community begins repurposing the stewardship of your institutional structures as a Christ-Commons, you will find that your ministry begins to focus even more on the flourishing of kingdom life. Life-transforming connections with God, each other, the world, and creation will enliven your church's participation with God in God's reconciling mission. As a Christ-Commons you are freed to see your communal life together as providing vital life-supporting services. Often we think of life support as medical services in a moment of physical or psychological crisis; certainly our institutional churches provide such services, but Christ-Commons take a more proactive role in supporting life. Christ-Commons actively support life by contextually retelling God's ongoing story of redemption, enacting this drama in Holy Communion and baptism, and reorienting the life of the faith community toward others through worship (toward God) and service (toward other people and creation). Christ-Commons provide biblical teaching, theologies, books, resources, liturgy, education, music, art, and so on, but the most important support these structures offer is the stewardship of space that encourages clustering in Christ to flourish.

Christ-Commons steward their structures in a similar way that a party committee plans for a dance. The committee thoughtfully prepares and decorates the gym, brings in a DJ with contextually appropriate music, provides ample refreshments, and chaperones the dance. But they can't make people dance.

Christ-Commons cultivate fertile soil for new life. The structures and forms they steward provide embodied contexts in which people join God in God's work of the re-creation of all things. In a very real way Christ-Commons function as localized and contextual expressions of the relational reign of God. Christ-Commons do not exist simply for the sake of the Christ-Commons but exist to foster lived life in the way of Jesus. Christ-Commons till the soil so the organic social and spiritual life of the community yields abundance. Thus the Christ-Commons may be best understood as a support structure for living Christ-Clusters (the subject of our next chapter), but we are wise not to mistake the connective structure for the whole church; body and soul form the dance of life.

The size of a church is not that important within this networked paradigm; what's more important is its connectivity. Whether your church is a megachurch with twenty thousand members or a house church with twenty, the structural issues remain: stewarding your structure so kingdom connections thrive. The church exists in relationship, by relationship, and for relationship. We exist to connect people with God, one another, and with creation in continuity with the capacious narrative of Scripture. Sometimes this means connecting people with a narrative so big and so beautiful that their lives find new meaning, redemption, and hope. Sometimes it might mean connecting people with others whom you personally wouldn't choose to connect with. Sometimes this may even mean helping people who are a vital part of your church connect to a different faith community or ministry even at great cost to your own ministry. And we can do this because every local Christ-Commons understands it is dynamically linked together in God's connective kingdom. The church doesn't exist simply to propagate the church, rather the local church exists as a local expression of the reality of God's networked kingdom.

Have you ever found yourself saying or thinking, "I'd love the church if it weren't for all the people"? We all know that to invite or even encourage relational connections is also to invite conflict. Every person in your community has a unique story filled with beauty and sorrow, hopes realized and not, and different beliefs, convictions, and values. So when we come together, we can expect sparks to fly. The metaphor of the catalytic converter enables us to reimagine how Christ-Commons create a connective environment that transforms these "sparks" into new life.

> People do not fear change, people fear loss.[5]
>
> Sharron Parks

Christ-Commons as Catalytic Converters

"Catalysis" is the process in which the rate of a chemical reaction is increased by means of a chemical substance known as a catalyst. Basically, a catalyst gets things going; maybe it's the butterfly flapping its wings in Brazil, or maybe it's the college student in your church who loves Christ and the world but is having a difficult time with church structure as she's experienced it. While a catalyst sparks transformation, Christ-Commons steward convective space for that transformation to thrive.

Somewhere between your car's motor and its exhaust pipe, your catalytic converter provides the environment for a chemical reaction wherein toxic combustion by-products are converted to less toxic substances. That's what catalytic converters do. The goal of the catalytic converter is to exist in such a way that the toxic energy that comes its way can get linked with the necessary resources so that the potentially toxic energy is relationally transformed.

Toxic energy can be overt or subtle. Jim Carlson, a pastor friend of mine in Spokane, recently shared his story of subtle toxins in the church he was pastoring and how those toxins were converted. As Jim told it, the church he was pastoring, which had a long history, had plateaued in nearly every way. The community was filled with good, faithful people, and, though there were fewer children and more grey hair, worship was lively and they were serving their community; giving was consistent and all-in-all it was a relatively stable, healthy church.

Jim learned of a church planter who was beginning a new work just down the road, so Jim called him up. Jim and the church planter ended up getting coffee. That cup of java turned into a friendship. Sometime later, as the two pastors were talking, they began to explore the possibility of bringing their two faith communities together for a joint worship service and a shared meal. Eventually they did. The service and meal provided a much-needed intergenerational connection for the two faith communities. In fact, the gathering was such a hit that they made it a regular occurrence.

And then one evening, when the well-established church was hosting, the children of the church plant were in fine form: running around the building, laughing, and having way too much fun in the house of God. The pastor of the long-established church stood up, hushed the adults inviting them to stop and listen, letting the sounds of the children wash over them . . . it hadn't been that long ago that the joyful sound of children had permeated their building. But that was then. Jim said, "Tears began rolling down the cheeks of one of the older women. It seemed that something was being set in motion."

The leadership of the two churches began to meet. They developed a mutual relationship and began to pray together, wondering if their connection might be a kingdom opportunity. After months of discernment, the established church unanimously voted to move in the direction of life: giving their beloved building to the new church with no strings attached to ensure the decision could not be reversed. They didn't stop there. The established congregation also voted to blend their ecclesial identity with the new church, essentially voting themselves out of existence. The established faith community adopted the mission of the newer church and joined it, forming what might be understood as a "blended church family." Pastor Jim stayed to help with the transition but stayed only long enough to ensure the blending of the church families would thrive. Jim is a real-life example of a pastor daringly stewarding a Christ-Commons toward networked life by choosing life over self-preservation, giving up life in order to find it.

Christ-Commons function as catalytic converters, stewarding their connective space so that potential "toxins," like a plateaued community or monogenerational community, can be transformed unto life abundant. As you reflect on the vitality of your Christ-Commons, are you aware of any potential toxins, whether subtle like Jim's or more overt? How might your church catalytically create space for the conversion of that energy toward life? Christ-Commons dare to imagine kingdom opportunities in face of conflict; we call it redemption.

> To perceive the world differently, to see it as infused with God, is to imagine the world as an embryo in the womb of God's love.[6]
>
> Jeff Cook

Now that we have a working understanding of Christ-Commons and glimpsed their connective function, we turn our attention to the role of pastor as a "Network Ecologist." Then we will consider the implications of this networked vision for authority ministry in God's connective kingdom.

The Pastor as Network Ecologist

In an earlier chapter we considered connective leaders by learning from network hubs. The parable of Google enabled us to see how connective leaders proactively link people to the meaning-making connections they seek. A network ecologist and a hub are not the same thing; although pastors do provide links, they also serve a unique ecological function within a Christ-Commons. Pastoring a Christ-Commons is like serving as a network ecologist. The network ecologist's primary concern is tending, cultivating, and caring for an environment so that accessible and sustainable kingdom linking thrives and hindrances to Christ-connections are mitigated. Network ecologists are mindful of the connective space necessary for the process of the catalytic conversation of potentially toxic energies that inevitably arise when lives bump into each other. Within this networked kingdom paradigm, pastors of Christ-Commons curate connective space.

Pastors are like the party planning committee preparing the gym for the dance. Pastors don't make transformation happen; neither can they control who connects or how they connect. Pastors humbly steward connective space so that people in our communities see themselves as participants with God in God's grand story of redemption. Switching metaphors, pastors of Christ-Commons are like farmers. No farmer can make a crop grow. Farmers work the soil so it is nutrient rich; they irrigate, select seed, and maintain equipment; and they pray, knowing that their primary work is stewarding the conditions for God to produce life.

Ecologists focus their energies not only on understanding living systems but also on the sustainable care of them. (In chapter 9 we'll explore network ecology even further.) Pastors as network ecologists seek to understand and sustainably care for the living system that is the church. They keep their eyes open for anything that might inhibit the flourishing of life while faithfully seeking to steward the conditions that promote life. Network ecologists do all this while understanding that their Christ-Commons is part of God's bigger connective kingdom. This is liberating, for it frees pastors from the feeling that they must provide the optimal growth conditions for everyone with whom they connect.

When we first started our house church (a small Christ-Commons), I worked diligently to get first-time guests to our community to connect with others in our group with the hope that they join "us." But as I began learning more about network theory and began to see that our Christ-Commons was a small part of God's much bigger vision, my approach to those first-time guests began to change. I began conversations with them by seeking to understand who they were, what some of their hopes for their lives were. I'd try to learn a bit about what their prior experiences of churches had been and how they imagined contributing to the shape of a faith community with the gift of their presence. Since these were conversations, I often ended up sharing some of my story and some of the narrative of our faith community. Sometimes after such conversations, the person sensed our community was the right place for them, and sometimes I had the privilege of helping the person find another Christ-Commons that better matched their place in their journey of following in the way of Christ.

I began to see that helping a person make a connection that best fit who they were and what they understood as their "calling," or some of their hopes, was an important part of my role as a network ecologist, as a pastor. No local church can be all things to all people, and we are fools to think otherwise. Each local church has a unique narrative and uniquely embodies the gospel of Jesus in its unique context. The primary mission of a Christ-Commons is not to get people to become members of one's local church but to advance God's kingdom. And in the networked kingdom paradigm, one of the most meaningful and effective ways of advancing the *shalom* of God is to weave a tapestry of kingdom connections, better enabling the person, family, or community to find fullness of life. In fact, this is one of the lessons we're learning from Google: that our greatest "power" is not accumulating links to ourselves but helping others connect meaningfully to what they need most. Discernment is needed to know when we are that primary link or when to serve as a matchmaker; after all, in a networked kingdom, when one person makes that vital connection, the entire network benefits.

The connective pastors of Christ-Commons are less concerned about assimilating people into their institution and more concerned with helping people find the meaningful connections they are seeking.

Where's the Authority?

Pastoring as a network ecologist is about stewarding an environment in such a way that people find and live into their personal and clustered callings and ministries in such a way that traditional hierarchies are flattened. This flattening of traditional hierarchies signals another way that God's connective kingdom provides a much-needed corrective lens to the church's understanding of authority. I am mindful that discussion of "church authority" can be rather controversial, yet we're all too aware of the damage done in and through the church as a result of our misuse of authority. So I am compelled to lean into this discussion believing that a more networked vision of authority may better enable us to steward our presence, power, and resources so that life can abound.

Almost all of our institutional structures, our Christ-Commons, have persons holding positions of authority. Depending on your tradition, you might have pastors, elders, bishops, a pontiff, or others.

114

These roles have authority over the functions of network ecologists. A pastor serves as network ecologist for a local indigenous Christ-Commons; the district superintendent or bishop serves as a regional network ecologist for local pastors; and so on. Each person holding a position of authority at any level in an institution functions to steward an ecology of connection for those in their care. And each of these positions play important roles in the ongoing process of stewarding their respective church traditions.

From a networked kingdom perspective, authority for ministry does not flow from the person with the positional title, nor does it flow from the faith community. It doesn't even flow from continuity with one's historic Christian tradition. "Authority" is generally understood as a claim of legitimacy, which serves as justification for action or the use of power. Where does the church look to justify any action? Certainly not to people or our own church structures; we look to Christ. From a networked perspective, authority resides in the mission of the network. As such, authoritative action is not judged by edict but by furthering the mission of the living system. Authority is revealed, not held. Networked authority is proven to be authentic by the realization of the missional identity of the network.

Any claim to Christian authority is understood by looking at the mission of God as seen in Jesus Christ. It is with this fervent belief that our prophets and reformers challenged the positional powers of their day. Our primary identity is as children of God, not Baptist, Lutheran, Orthodox, Republican, Democrat, or Independent. Our authority does not come from these human institutions but from God, and authoritative claim or action is authenticated by its resonance with God and God's mission.

Moments before Jesus returned to his Father, he told his followers, "All authority has been given to me. Therefore go and make disciples" (Matt. 28:18–19). Christian authority in ministry is imparted from Christ and authenticated in missional congruence. As we join God in the ministry of reconciliation, God's authority is imparted to us as the Holy Spirit's empowering presence. True authority is participation with God in God's mission of the redemption of all things and the re-creation of heaven and earth. We can test our participation with God in God's mission. Did life as seen in Jesus Christ flourish? Or was life in the way of Christ diminished? Or in the words of Jesus to inmate John the Baptist, "Are the blind seeing? Are the lame walking? Are the lepers cured? Do the deaf hear? Are the dead raised to life? Is the Good News being preached to the poor?" (Luke 7:18–23, my paraphrase). Are we doing justice, are we loving mercy, and are we walking humbly with our God?

The Eastern Orthodox Church has a helpful way of thinking about networked authority, often referred to as "the conscience of the Church," which stresses the consensus of Christians. The thought is that the conscience of the network of Christians is the conscience of our networked Christ-Commons with a deep belief that the Holy Spirit is active in leading people to fullness in Christ. From a network perspective, authority for ministry resides in God and God's mission.

Where do you look for authority in ministry? Can you imagine what it might mean to liberate the imaginations of the people in your faith community to daringly orient their lives around active participation with God in God's reconciling mission? I both love this question and feel the weight of it. For daring to do so means that the Christ-Commons must not shrink back from shaping the kingdom imaginations of the community.

> God is in the business of inventively and creatively calling forth communities to think and rethink our doctrines of the church.[7]
>
> Michael Jinkins

The church as a Christ-Commons. The pastor as a network ecologist. Authority for life and ministry as rooted in God and God's reconciling mission. Looking at the local church through the lens of God's connective kingdom daringly invites us to rethink and reimagine all that we are and do in light of the mission of God. This chapter has focused on the institutional structures of the church, its body. In the next chapter we will focus on the church's organic social and spiritual clustering: its soul.

Recommended Resources for Further Reflection

Arie De Geus, *The Living Company* (Cambridge, MA: Harvard Business School Press, 2002).

116

Peter M. Senge, *The Fifth Discipline: The Art and Practice of the Learning Organization* (New York: Doubleday, 2006).

Questions for Personal Reflection or Small Group Conversation

- When you hear the word "institution," what images or metaphors come to mind? How does the idea of the "Christ-Commons" inform your imagination for your institution(s)?
- How are you already stewarding the connective space in the ministry or relational networks of your life? How might your ministry be enhanced by envisioning yourself as a network ecologist?
- In your experience, how is authority used in your life and in your ministry? How do you understand authority in the life of the church?

7

Christ-Clusters

Reimagining the Soul of the Local Church

True religion is real living; living with all one's soul, with all one's goodness and righteousness.[1]

Albert Einstein

If you're anything like me, sometimes you can get so close to an idea that you lose sight of why you were drawn to it in the first place. The other day, for example, I was looking for my #2 Robertson screwdriver (square bit). I went out to our garage to retrieve it from its rightful place on my peg-board above the workbench and . . . horror of all horrors, it wasn't there. I searched high and low for the stupid thing. Before long I'd cleaned off my entire workbench, rehanging other tools I'd used without returning them to their proper place (a pattern, maybe?). I even installed a couple of extra hooks and rearranged some existing hooks for easier access. Next I moved on to my shelving, which I straightened and tidied, throwing out some of the unnecessary junk that garages tend to collect. I sorted out what could be recycled and hauled out a few loads of trash. Finally, after pulling my car out, sweeping the floor, and pulling my car back in, I went inside the house, pleased with my nice clean garage. Once inside—you saw it coming—the incomplete project that sent me to the garage was still there, and I still didn't have my #2 Robertson screwdriver.

We've probably all had experiences like that; we get so caught up in the urgency of a moment that we forget the bigger picture. For pastors, or network ecologists, there is no end to the vocation of ministry: administrative tasks, worship preparation, hospital visits, and websites to update (and we can't forget the seemingly omnivorous committee meetings), let alone fostering a life of prayer and attending to the needs of one's personal health and home life. Most days we love our churches, so it is relatively easy for us to order our lives around caring for those in our communities. We help people find meaningful connections with the narrative of God in Scripture, and lean into our liturgical traditions so that God is worshiped authentically in our context, not to mention stewarding the limited resources of our community so that the world is blessed and our local needs are met. Truth be told, the many responsibilities required for faithful stewardship of Christ-Commons can at times cause us to lose sight of God's bigger picture.

God's bigger picture reminds us that the effective administrative leadership of a local church is not an end in itself. Churches exist so that the identity of the people gathering together, both as networked persons and as a community, are being formed by the good news in such a way that they actually go about their lives living in the way of Christ. Churches don't exist just for the faithful administration of the sacraments, as important as that is, but as local, indigenous communities giving expression to the already-and-not-yet reality of God's reign on earth as it is in heaven.

The previous chapter looked at our institutional church life through the lens of God's connective kingdom: the body of the church. Now we focus on the church's soul, while always remembering that body and soul are inseparably one. A networked understanding of God's kingdom invites us to imagine the soul of the church as Christ-Clustering.

> The cell is the microcosm of life for in its origin, nature and continuity resides the entire problem of biology.[2]
>
> William S. Beck

Christ-Clusters

God's networked kingdom finds expression as people cluster together, centered in Christ, living in the way of Jesus. A "Christ-Cluster" is a relational grouping of people who are responsible for discrete, Holy Spirit-guided and cluster-determined cellular functions. Christ-Clustering is a dynamic, communal expression of God's good news that finds tangible expression in service, justice, and love. Christ-Clustering happens when people unite together to give away what they most need. Before we consider Christ-Clustering as the people of God, let's consider what we can learn about clustering from cellular biology.

Think of your own physical body for a moment. At the microscopic level, we are all composed of cells. Look at yourself in a mirror; what you see is about ten trillion cells divided into about two hundred different types. Our muscles are made of muscle cells, our livers of liver cells, and there are even very specialized types of cells that make the enamel for our teeth or the clear lenses in our eyes. Wonder of wonders, those different cell types were not present when you were conceived. At the moment of conception, each of us was a single living cell called a pronucleus. Within moments of conception, cellular division begins. By the time you were seventy-two hours old, you were eight cells; after four days, about one hundred cells; and by adulthood, you reached ten trillion (10,000,000,000,000) cells. The process of cellular division (mitosis) begins with one cell that divides to make an exact duplicate, yet somehow we end up with roughly two hundred different cell types. God, who seems to love story, relationship, and transformation, has created cellular life in such a way that when cells divide based on their relationship, connectedness, and context, they become a liver cell, or a skin cell, or a blood cell. The context and the unique set of cellular connections seem to summon forth the new cell's type.

Likewise, Christ-Clusters are small groups of people united in Christ, living responsively to the invitation for the gospel to be uniquely embodied in their context. These groups are not what we typically think of when we hear the word "church." They are fluid and culturally responsive. They self-organize and dissipate when their "cellular function" is complete.

121

Christ-Cluster in God's Networked Kingdom

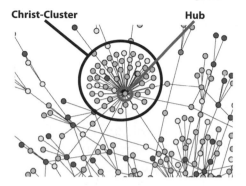

One afternoon, a group of friends from our house church were hanging out at a coffee shop when a college student who had recently begun to participate in our faith community walked in. She joined the others and they were soon lost in conversation. Since the coffee shop was close to the college student's home, she invited them over to continue their conversation and make dinner together. Not long after getting to her home, the phone rang and very quickly the group knew that something was seriously wrong.

As it turned out, the woman's brother (who was also a college student, but up in Alaska) had just found out that he had been exposed to the HIV/AIDS virus. He was terrified and alone, and wanted to be with his sister when he got the test results back. The group responded exactly the way one would hope a Christ-Cluster would respond. Some prayed and some finished preparing dinner. One of them pulled out his laptop and credit card and began to make flight arrangements for her brother to fly down. A couple of the women stayed overnight, offering the gift of presence.

When his plane arrived in Seattle, the group drove her to the airport to pick him up and spent the better part of the next few days together. A few members of the group even booked time off from work to support him as he got the test results back from the clinic. And when the test results came back negative, they all celebrated the good news. That is what Christ-Clustering looks like. And that kind of "cellular life" is like the soul of the church: people being God's good news in very natural and peculiar ways. This little group dynamically self-organized when presented with a real need and dissipated when their "cellular function" was complete.

At the beginning of the book, I introduced you to Lyndon Harris, the priest at St. Paul's on the day the airplanes were hijacked and flown into the Twin Towers. As you remember, scores of volunteers just showed up to do whatever they could do to help. Clustering together, they spontaneously formed search teams, grilled burgers, gave massages to weary rescue workers, created message boards to help people find missing loved ones, and all kinds of other vital services. This too is what Christ-Clustering looks like.

You might be thinking, "But surely not all those volunteers serving at Ground Zero were followers of Christ. How can that be Christ-Clustering?" For people whose lives are being shaped by the good news of God's reconciling work, Christ-Clustering is the active participation with God in the flourishing of life. It is, as Henry Blackaby has taught, seeing where God is at work and joining in.[3] As soon as an opportunity for blessing others, or standing in the face of injustice, presents itself, that is the invitation for Christ-Clustering. In this way Christ-Clustering is active participation with the Holy Spirit and with whoever else is willing to help in realizing God's dream for creation.

Spontaneous Clustering

Christ-Clusters self-organize for gospel embodiment based on relationship and context in concert with the Holy Spirit. We can't form a Christ-Cluster artificially; clustering just happens when people are centered in Christ and responsive to their surroundings. Christ-Clusters are not the same as small group ministries. Small groups are a form, or structure, like a mini Christ-Commons. Christ-Clustering is dynamic and responsive to a particular moment. You can't plan for clustering, but you can prepare by training yourself and those in your community to recognize God's work.

I have no doubt you have similar stories to the ones above. They are to be savored, for such stories remind us of the living nature of life with God, which always manifests itself in love for and service to others and creation. My guess is that for many of us, stories like this played a part in our choice to follow in the way of Jesus.

Christ-Clusters are not an institution, nor are they an organization. You can't make a cluster happen; they just happen. These
are spontaneous moments where the kingdom of God is realized in
our midst. They are movements of solidarity, justice, compassion,
humility, grace, and love when we unite in the Spirit of God, express-
ing the very life for which we are created.

After a Christ-Clustering experience, there can often be a desire
to formalize the process so that it can be repeated. Entire ministries
are sometimes created in the wake of such outpourings of God's
Spirit through a Christ-Cluster. Of course the development of new
ministries can be a good and beautiful thing. However, the transition from a cluster experience to an institutional ministry can be
challenging. It reminds me a bit of Jesus's disciples wanting to build
three tents on the mountain when Jesus became radiant and spoke
with Moses and Elijah. The priesthood of all believers is realized
when Christ-Clustering happens. Everyone belongs and everyone
contributes what they can. A networked kingdom paradigm views
cellular functions as any form of communication[4] linking or bridging toward Christ.

These Christ-Clusters are socially constructed realities guided by
the Holy Sprit.[5] Yet it is vital that we recognize they are more than
mere human social constructs, for God is the center and participating
shaper of these social constructs. As we are in Christ and Christ is in
us, our dialectical social interactions legitimate our clusters as Christian or, more explicitly, Christlike. To put it another way, drawing from
the previous chapter, what legitimates such clustering as authentic
Christian ministry is its congruence with the mission of God.

Christ-Commons Foster an Environment for Clustering

We won't spend much time on this since the previous chapter focused
on the institutional structures of the church. But it seems wise to
spend just a moment reviewing Christ-Commons now that we have
a clearer picture of Christ-Clustering. The structures, teaching, and
practices of our churches dance together in the formation of our
new identity as children of God. Our new identity is expressed in
the many relationships and contexts in which we live. In a sense,

Christ-Commons steward a connective space, liberating and empowering people to embody God's life-giving good news. Our Christ-Commons foster an environment where this kind of clustering is more likely to happen than not. It's not that this kind of dynamic clustering only happens in the confines of the church's structure, though it does happen there too. Most often Christ-Clustering happens in the day-to-day life of normal people who are open to active participation with God in loving their neighbors, welcoming strangers, taking a stand for justice, extending grace, and humbly bearing witness to the truth of Christ they have experienced.

People in all churches can do this. Even the most traditional or rigid church structures or traditions can learn to foster an environment in which everyone can cluster in God's networked kingdom. Christ-Clustering groups of people can self-organize based on relationship and context for gospel embodiment in concert with the Holy Spirit.

Christ-Clustering: The Soul of the Local Church

This chapter's subtitle, "Reimagining the Soul of the Local Church," suggests that this kind of clustering shapes the identity of local churches. The soul, as I am using the term, is the spirit or consciousness that animates the body. This Christ-Clustering activity is what animates the institutional life of our churches. When the people in our church gather together for worship and they know that they have personally participated with God in God's mission, the "We" of our faith community is enlivened. Our attentiveness to God's capacious narrative in Scripture is heightened, for we know that we are part of God's ongoing story.

Christ-Clusters are the soul of the local church. It is through this discrete, Holy Spirit-inspired clustering action that the way of Christ finds expression in the lives of the people in our churches. And it is not just for the people in our churches; the clustering effect serves to bless others, and works to end suffering for others. Christianity is far more than adherence to a book or a system of beliefs, and it is more than an individual moral code. Christianity is a reorientation toward the fullness of life as revealed in Jesus of Nazareth.

The pattern of organization of any system, living or non-living, is the configuration of relationships among the system's components that determines the system's essential characteristics. In other words, certain relationships must be present for something to be recognized as—say—a chair, a bicycle, or a tree. That configuration of relationships that gives a system its essential characteristics is what we mean by its pattern of organization.[6]

Fritjof Capra

Christ's Living Church: Body and Soul

One of the challenges many church practitioners face is the seeming discrepancy between the vision of church as seen in Scripture and the established church structures of today. The preponderance of biblical metaphors for God's people throughout Scripture suggests that the church is a living reality. Metaphors like Christ's body, a city on a hill, flock of sheep, bride, holy nation, vineyard, a people; these are not images of some static religious institution but of something much more dynamic.

I've tried to stress that the body and soul cannot be separated in the church any more than they can be separated in a person. Life is the unity of body and soul. Through the dynamic union of Christ-Commons and Christ-Clustering, the local church lives. The Christ-Commons provides form for clustering, while the Christ-Clustering animates the Christ-Commons.

There is a fluidity here, but also something of a tension. Maybe that tension is why we so often try to separate the two. Albert Barabási, the physicist whose research team discovered scale-free networks, speaks to this tension:

Gases are simple: Molecules fly in empty space, taking notice of each other only when they bounce into one another. Crystals are the opposite but relatively simple, too: Molecules hold hands tightly to create a perfectly rigid lattice. Liquids, however, strike a delicate balance between these two extremes. The attractive forces that keep the water molecules together are not strong enough to coerce them into a rigid order. Trapped between order and chaos, water molecules participate in a majestic dance in which some molecules come together, form

126

small and somewhat ordered groups, move together, and in no time break apart to join other molecules forming yet other groups.[7]

Through a description of the molecular structure of H_2O, Barabási beautifully describes the incarnational reality that is the now-and-not-yet kingdom of God: God's Holy Spirit and God's people gather in a majestic, fluid dance, forming somewhat ordered groups that move together and then break apart, only to form yet other groups.

In a similar vein, theologian Jürgen Moltmann writes, "A thing is alive only when it contains contradiction in itself and is indeed the power of holding the contradiction within itself and enduring it. It is not reflection, recalling man's own subjectivity from its social realization, that brings him back to possibilities and therewith his freedom, but this is done only by the hope which leads him to expend himself and at the same time makes him grasp continually new possibilities from the expected future."[8]

A church is only alive when it contains contradiction in itself, and it is indeed in the power of holding the contradiction—body and soul—within the church and enduring them that Christ's church lives and thrives. Our institutional churches are living structures. Granted, there are times that our institutional structures may seem to work against dynamic clustering, but it is in holding the tension that the church lives. Although institutions often have the look of fixed permanence, and equally as often present themselves as such, they are themselves living structures.

Arie de Geus describes four marks of organizations that signal that they are living realties. They are marked by,

1. Sensitivity to their environment, which is reflected in how they learn, adapt and change over time;
2. Cohesion and differentiated identity, which is seen in how they communicate their tradition as distinct;
3. Tolerance of some level of diversity within their own structures;
4. Success in administrative issues, as seen in their ability to steward its growth, finances, and organizational effectiveness.[9]

All four of these marks are evident in our churches. Institutions are structures and mechanisms of social order and cooperation governing the behavior of a set of individuals. As such it doesn't matter how formal or informal one's expression of church might be; it is an institution. And institutions are typically identified with a social purpose and relative permanence that transcends individual human lives and intentions. Although some of my friends in the avant-church world (simple churches, neomonastic communities, emerging churches, and missional churches) might balk at the thought of institutions, what they're often responding to is the tension of contextual ecclesial innovation rubbing shoulders with the larger traditions of the church. This tension is one of the great gifts of the church as it calls forth a fluid dance of individual persons, the local community of faith, and the historic tradition of the people of God. This dynamic tension both invites the individual to repentance and invites historic institutions to ongoing self-examination and reform. In fact, this tension underscores the fact that the church is a living community.

Seeing life through the paradigm of God's networked kingdom animates what can at first seem fixed. Since we've already seen that links are living, it should come as no surprise that this networked vision also helps us to see church structures as living. If Christ-Clusters are the soul of the church, then the institutional forms are the body of the church . . . what God has joined together let no person separate.

> A system is a network of interdependent components that work together to try to accomplish the aim of the system. A system must have an aim. Without the aim, there is no system.[10]
>
> W. Edwards Deming

Recommended Resources for Further Reflection

Ori Brafman and Rod A. Beckstrom, *The Starfish and the Spider: The Unstoppable Power of Leaderless Organizations* (New York: Portfolio, 2006).

Dietrich Bonhoeffer, *Life Together*, trans. John W. Doberstein (New York: Harper Collins, 1978).

Questions for Personal Reflection or Small Group Conversation

- At the beginning of the chapter we talked about how the business of life and ministry can sidetrack us from the big picture of ministry. How are you understanding that big picture and what practices are you developing to help you order your life around that vision?
- Share an experience of Christ-Clustering from your own life.
- Consider how you might steward your context so that such spontaneous clustering is even more likely to occur.

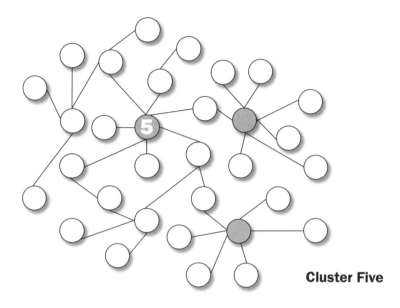

Connective Practices

In this final cluster of chapters, we look even more concretely at some of the practices for embodying missional linking.

We will begin by exploring the "Christ conjunctive," becoming an "*And*," boldly linking what had been separated. "*And'ing*" is participation with God in God's reconciling mission. We'll also consider the viral spread of the good news via the "sneeze effect."

Then we will look at network ecology and the importance of embracing the whole life cycle in the stewardship of our Christ-Commons. We will conclude by looking at spiritual formation as weaving a kingdom tapestry. We will see that networked spirituality holds both "centered" and "bounded set" visions of the Christian life.

Missional *And'ing*

The Sneeze Effect and the Viral Gospel

> Since you cannot do good to all, you are to pay special attention to those who, by the accidents of time, or place, or circumstances, are brought into closer connection with you.[1]
>
> Augustine

After giving a talk about missional *And'ing* (I'll define this in a moment) recently, I was sent an email with a Calvin and Hobbes comic strip attached. In the cartoon Calvin (the boy) was telling Hobbes (the tiger) how much he likes to "verb" words. Calvin says, "I take nouns and adjectives and use them as verbs. Remember when 'access' was a thing? Now it's something you *do*. It got verbed . . . Verbing weirds language." To which Hobbes replies, "Maybe we can eventually make language a complete impediment to understanding."

I certainly hope I am not making language a "complete impediment to understanding," but I do want to highlight the "conjunctive" action of living in the way of Christ. Missional "*And'ing*," as we will see in this chapter, is about living as an agent in God's mission of reconciliation.

133

God's mission as revealed in and through Christ is to bring fullness of life. The apostle Paul describes "fullness of life" and the mission of God through the church this way:

> What this means is that those who become Christians become new persons. They are not the same anymore, for the old life is gone. A new life has begun! All this newness of life is from God, who brought us back to himself through what Christ did. And God has given us the task of reconciling people to him. For God was in Christ, reconciling the world to himself, no longer counting people's sins against them. This is the wonderful message he has given us to tell others. We are Christ's ambassadors, and God is using us to speak to you. We urge you, as though Christ himself were here pleading with you, "Be reconciled to God!" (2 Cor. 5:17–20).

The missional focus of God's people is reconciliation. This is an inherently relational process of linking together those who have been separated. To be reconciled is to restore to friendship or harmony, to settle a conflict, to make consistent or congruous. Reconciliation does not mean that we come to complete agreement but rather choose relationship over separation. The emphasis of Paul's statement is on humans being reconciled with God; when our relationship with the Creator and sustainer of life is in harmony, then the possibility of joining God in God's own reconciling ministry flows naturally from it. We see this in Paul's own life.

Before Paul became the missionary apostle to the Gentiles, he was Saul, an anti-Christian crusader bent on arresting and helping execute Jesus's followers. But that was before Christ. And when a person is reconciled to God through Christ by the Holy Spirit, a person's vision of others begins to transform. We see this transformation in Paul as he becomes one of the greatest missional linkers of all time. His entire life is reoriented from defining himself against the other to defining himself as a reconciling agent of God's connected kingdom. Where once he focused his energies and passions on those things that tend to divide us, he began to see with God's connective vision. Consider Paul's *And'ing* words to the Galatian church:

> But the scripture says that the whole world is under the power of sin; and so the gift which is promised on the basis of faith in Jesus Christ

is given to those who believe. But before the time for faith came, the Law kept us all locked up as prisoners until this coming faith should be revealed. And so the Law was in charge of us until Christ came, in order that we might then be put right with God through faith. Now that the time for faith is here, the Law is no longer in charge of us. It is through faith that all of you are God's children in union with Christ Jesus. You were baptized into union with Christ, and now you are clothed, so to speak, with the life of Christ himself. So there is no difference between Jews *and* Gentiles, between slaves *and* free people, between men *and* women; you are all one in union with Christ Jesus. If you belong to Christ, then you are the descendants of Abraham and will receive what God has promised. (Gal. 3:22–29 GNT, emphasis mine)

Missional linking is marked by a kingdom imagination that, when confronted with "otherness," is able to see an *And'ing* in Christ; Jew *and* Gentile, slave *and* free, men *and* women, Republican *and* Democrat, modern *and* postmodern, left *and* right. The way of Christ is to become the *And*. God's mission, if you choose to live into it, is to boldly link where no one has linked before; this is the Christ-conjunction.

So then, no one should split apart what God has joined together.[2]

Jesus

Boldly Linking

And'ers are bold linkers. A node can feel safe and secure in its own cluster of safety; these clusters are little communities in which people are known and loved. But *And'ing* followers of Christ seek connection beyond their natural affective community.[3] In his book *The Cluetrain Manifesto*, David Weinberger describes missional linking using the term "hyperlinks." Weinberger writes:

[Hyperlinking] throws everyone into immediate connection with everyone else without the safety net of defined roles and authorities. . . . Conversations subvert hierarchy. Hyperlinks subvert hierarchy. Being a human being among others subverts hierarchy.[4]

Missional Linking

Having written extensively on the missional church, Darrell Guder of Princeton Theological Seminary says, "Connectional structures are missiologically essential to the apostolicity, catholicity, holiness and unity of the church."[5] Guder further stresses that "the movement toward missional connectedness should be centrifugal, starting from particular communities and expanding to the global dimensions of the church."[6] *And'ers* engage in missional centrifugal linking, moving beyond their affective Christ-Clusters to other nodes and clusters. This process of missional linking impacts the very being of the *And'er.* When we understand a person to be a networked person, we begin by understanding that we are socially constituted beings. Thus missional linking with any "other" node or cluster will also contribute to the ongoing "becoming" of the person.[7] What I'm saying is that any time we missionally link with the hope of a genuine *I & You* encounter, we can expect to be changed through the process of connecting. When we try to missionally connect without such openness to the other, a type of colonialism results.

The apostle Paul is very helpful in aiding our consideration of opening ourselves to genuine encounter with others, and his words to the church in Corinth reflect his *And'ing* strategy. In fact, his words may suggest that Paul's "being" was literally being shaped by the genuine encounters with others.

> When I am with the Jews, I become one of them so that I can bring them to Christ. When I am with those who follow the Jewish laws, I do the same, even though I am not subject to the law, so that I can bring them to Christ. When I am with the Gentiles who do not have the Jewish law, I fit in with them as much as I can. In this way, I gain their confidence and bring them to Christ. But I do not discard the law of God; I obey the law of Christ. When I am with those who are oppressed, I share their oppression so that I might bring them to Christ. Yes, I try to find common ground with everyone so that I might bring them to Christ. I do all this to spread the Good News, and in doing so I enjoy its blessings. (1 Cor. 9:20–23)

And'ers responding to an invitation from a Christ-Cluster's communal ethos to serve a linking function will position themselves in such a way that the safety of their own social construct is open to transformation for the hope of establishing links where none existed previously. God perfected missional linking in Christ: God incarnate. Missional linking facilitates change in the *And'ing* person. This only makes sense because any time a person with a networked identity has a genuine encounter with a person from a very different networked identity link, both are transformed as together they form a new *We* identity. This transformation within the *And'er* inevitably introduces disruption in that person's affective cluster(s). Many of us have seen this when a friend returns from a mission trip and they are simply different. Their perspectives have broadened as they have been shaped, maybe even transformed, through relational connections.

There are a few missional *And'ing* practices that actually contribute to the *We* identity of God's people. The first practice of missional linking is what Paul is most known for: intentionally seeking to be in relation with the "other." The second form of missional *And'ing* practice is hospitality, where we intentionally welcome the stranger.

These two practices provide an *And'ing* perspective for nearly every relational encounter imaginable. Either we get to serve as a host who welcomes the stranger, or we get to intentionally seek to form a relationship with the other. Once a link is established, a new *We* is formed and our networks, which may have been separated by multiple degrees of separation, are now linked. It seems so straightforward, and in fact it is. How are we seeking to form connections with the people we encounter and those who encounter us?

> Life begets life. Energy becomes energy. It is by spending oneself that one becomes rich.[8]
>
> Sarah Bernhardt

The Strength of Weak Links

Let's begin by looking more closely at how networking informs our intentional linking with others. One of the surprising discoveries of complexity theory came from Mark Granovetter of Johns Hopkins University. He proved that a strong network is made up of many weak links. In fact, a network comprised of many weak links is stronger and more enduring than a network made up of fewer but stronger links.

Imagine a person who is just beginning to walk in the way of Christ and is being discipled by one close friend. Then imagine that the person's only connection is their mentor with no other support, no other resources, no books, no churches, no other friends, no organizational structures. Now imagine tragedy strikes, severing the link between the mentor and the follower. What is likely to happen to the new disciple? Clearly, the new disciple is cut off; the person is left alone without a life-giving network. It's an extreme example, because we instinctively know that multiple links form a web of life-giving support.

Consider another example. This time think of a network of highways on an island with only one ten-lane bridge connecting it to the mainland. Network theory shows us that even though the island has a large bridge connecting it to the mainland, the network is at great risk of losing connection. The network of roads would be stronger if it had multiple bridges—even if the bridges are smaller—because all it takes is one multicar accident, chemical spill, or hurricane to shut down the single bridge. And if the island only has one bridge, it would then be cut off from the mainland. Simply put, there is a better chance for the island to remain connected with two or more bridges. Robust and sustainable networks are composed of many links, even if the links are comparably weak.

In his article "The Strength of Weak Ties,"[9] Granovetter shows that the weak links between people serve as social bridges. A bridge facilitates connection to otherwise isolated units. It may have to span a deep chasm or a small brook, but any bridge is better than none.[10] In this sense, the strength of a link is relatively meaningless; a link is a link. Strong or weak, any link connects two otherwise unconnected entities.

Mark Buchanan says, "Notice that bridging links of this sort do not merely connect you to one other person. They are bridges into distant and otherwise quite alien social worlds."[11] These bridges simultaneously intertwine the *And'er* with the Christ-Cluster, the *And'er* with the "other," and the "other" with the Christ-Cluster.[12] The *And'er* who is inseparably linked to their Christ-Cluster is like the yeast that is kneaded through dough in Christ's parable; the "I'm in Christ/Christ in me," living, incarnational relationship is the gospel that spreads through the myriad of links that make up human existence.

The network understanding of the strength of weak links is very freeing for intentional missional engagement. Embracing the strength of weak links frees you from feeling the need to "fix" or convert the other, from the feeling that you must solve a problem, while simultaneously linking two formally disparate clusters together to move in the direction of mutual transformation. The strength of the weak link is that a new relationship is now formed between two people who are each webbed together in at least two different clusters. Those two clusters now cross-pollinate. Both begin to be transformed by the encounter. Christianity as a Jewish sect, for instance, was transformed by Paul and others linking to Rome. Rome was transformed, eventually making Christianity its state religion. And what's stunning is that Paul was just a regular networked person like you and me, intentionally seeking to boldly link where no one had linked before. In many ways, as Paul went about his life open to the possibility of genuine encounter, he virally spread the good news of fullness of life in Christ.

Mutually transforming relationship
of *And'er*/Christ-Cluster/The Other

And'er   **Christ-Cluster**

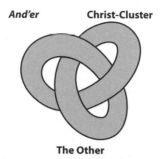

The Other

Weak links are often of greater importance than strong links because they act as the crucial ties that sew the social network together.[13]

Mark Buchanan

Living the Viral Gospel

John Barry's book *The Great Influenza* chronicles the epic story of the deadliest plague in history. "In the winter of 1918, at the height of World War I, history's most lethal influenza virus erupted in an Army camp in Kansas, moved east with American troops, then exploded, killing as many as 100 million people worldwide. It killed more people in twenty-four weeks than AIDS has killed in twenty-four years, more in a year than the Black Death killed in a century."[14] In biological terms, a virus is a submicroscopic infectious agent that is unable to grow or reproduce outside a host cell. Once introduced into a host cell, it grows, multiplies, and spreads to those with whom the host is linked. Of course, viruses are not just biological; there are computer viruses, fashion trends, and hit TV shows, as well as relational or social viruses.

Of the numerous writers who have shaped our imaginations around the social virus, none have been more widely read than Malcolm Gladwell. In his wildly successful book *The Tipping Point*, Gladwell describes three characteristics of a social virus, which I want us to consider as we explore God's connective kingdom. The first characteristic of a social virus that Gladwell highlights is "contagiousness"; the second, little causes with big effects; and third, dramatic, not gradual, change. Let's begin by considering the contagiousness of the good news.

The Contagiousness of Good News

It's hard to keep good news to yourself. When a couple who has been hoping for a child discover they are expecting, or when a young man proposes marriage and she accepts, or when you receive that promotion that you've been working and hoping for—this is news that has to be shared. That's exactly what the gospel is like. It's like a woman who calls her friends together to celebrate after finding a valuable coin, or like a shepherd inviting his friends to rejoice after finding the lamb he feared he'd lost, or like the father who throws a party after the return of his prodigal son (Luke 15). When good news breaks into our lives, we simply can't keep it to ourselves.

Good news is like a breaking news story that inverts the direction of our lives by redeeming what we thought was hopeless. "I thought my marriage was over and then . . ."; "I feared my life partner was going to die of cancer and then. . . ." When we talk about the gospel as good news, we are talking about the in-breaking story of God that can transform our lives here and now and for all eternity. Good news transforms us from mourning loss to celebrating life; good news frees us from the weight of despair to the joy of new hope, from the downward spiral of apathy to meaning and purpose. And with the good news of the incarnation of God—as seen in the life, death, and resurrection of Christ that makes possible genuine *I & You* encounters with the living God—we're not just talking about having our sins forgiven. Though that is certainly good news, we're talking about the redemption and re-creation of the entire universe; we're talking about the glorious hope and already-but-not-yet reality of all things—yes, all things—being reconciled unto God. This is the contagious good news of God's networked kingdom.

Good News: Little Causes and Big Effects

One of the most striking aspects of the good news is the way God seems to delight in using small, insignificant things and people to bring about fantastic transformations—from Jesus's birth to an unwed teenager in a rural town where he only had a feed trough for a crib, to the thousands of women and men who have faithfully lived into their understanding and experience of the gospel so that it has been passed on to you and to me. I've already touched on the idea of the Butterfly Effect, which mathematically proved that the flapping of a butterfly's wings in Brazil could redirect a tornado in Texas, but we all have stories highlighting God's redemption of small things that have big effects. Maybe it was the grandmother who prayed for you; the uncle who sent you a check out of the blue when you were in college; a brief conversation with a homeless woman; or a poem you read—if you listen to your own story, or the stories of some of your friends and family, you will likely hear a lot of little connections having big effects.

As a seven- or eight-year-old, I was playing in my friend's horse pasture when he looked up and pointed at an airliner flying over-head. He commented that the plane was full of people with families, homes, and destinations. That thought had never occurred to me before—other people were like me; they too had families, they too had homes, they too had dreams of places they'd like to go.

If it's true that seemingly simple, little things can have big effects, then it's wise to ponder how we steward our presence. Missional *And'ers* live by the motto, "You never know!" You never know what effects might be born of even your smallest connection—be it a hope-filled conversation or disparaging look, movement of solidarity or act of defiance, spirit of arrogance or humble confession. Who we are and how we steward our presence with others will impact others in ways we simply can't imag-ine. When missional *And'ers* live with this motto, every interpersonal exchange can be seen as an opportunity to participate in the ending of suffering and an opportunity to encourage fullness of life.

Good News and Dramatic Change

The phrase "the tipping point" was first used in sociology in the late 1950s by political scientist Morton Grodzins to describe the "white flight" as many Caucasian Americans began moving out of the nation's urban core. Malcolm Gladwell picked up the term, broadening its meaning to refer to change that does not happen gradually but rather at one dramatic moment. The tipping point refers to any process in which, beyond a certain point, the rate at which the process proceeds increases dramatically. Take the publication of a new novel. The book is released, sales trickle in. Then Oprah raves about the novel on her show and it becomes an "instant bestseller." When we speak of tipping points, we're talking about network phenomena, moments when the collective consciousness of a social network dramatically shifts. When Rosa Parks refused to move to the back of the bus, America experienced a tipping point with regard to racial segregation.

Typically we don't use "tipping point" to refer to individual change, but there are some striking similarities. Sometimes a person will speak of having a sudden awakening, or a moment of *gestalt*, or even a conversion. Throughout this project we're coming to appreciate the dynamic interconnection and interanimation of individual nodes, the nodes' affective clusters, and the network as a whole. I believe the global church is approaching a tipping point in our understanding of the gospel. Philip Jenkins has documented the shift in Christian influence and numbers from the northern hemisphere to the global south. And from every continent there are church leaders and thinkers calling for us to rediscover the whole gospel for the whole world—not a partial gospel, not an individualized gospel, not a colonizing gospel but the good news.

The Sneeze Effect

Living the viral gospel is a little like sneezing. A sneeze (or sternutation) is a semiautonomous, convulsive expulsion of air from the lungs, most commonly caused by foreign particles irritating the nasal mucosa. Sneezing is a natural, albeit virtually uncontrollable, part of breathing. Did you know that a cough releases an explosive charge of air that moves at speeds up to sixty miles per hour, and that sneezes can exceed one hundred miles per hour? Or that after only thirty seconds of use, a handkerchief has been found to contain fifteen thousand germs?[15] Whatever is in you, you will share it with others. This is the wonder and power of an *And'ing* vision of God's networked kingdom. As you go about your life, you can't help but infect those you come in contact with, and you just never know what impact your presence, words, or actions might have. God bless you as you sneeze.

Sneeze Effect (photograph by Andrew Davidhazy)

Hold that thought as we look at one of the often misunderstood and misused statements from Jesus's Sermon on the Mount. Toward the end of Matthew 5 is Jesus's call for his hearers to be perfect as the heavenly Father is perfect. Not long ago, I spent a significant amount of time sitting with this sermon, letting it soak in, and this statement became a hope-filled statement for me. I was stunned by its relational tone. Read it for yourself:

> You have heard that the law of Moses says, "Love your neighbor" and hate your enemy. But I say, love your enemies! Pray for those who persecute you! In that way, you will be acting as true children of your Father in heaven. For he gives his sunlight to both the evil and the good, and he sends rain on the just and on the unjust, too. If you love only those who love you, what good is that? Even corrupt tax collectors do that much. If you are kind only to your friends, how are you different from anyone else? Even pagans do that. But you are to be perfect, even as your Father in heaven is perfect. (Matt. 5:44–48)

The context of Jesus's invitation to us to be perfect as God the Father is perfect is in our relationship with the "other"—even our enemies. This is truly a striking call for us to enter the world with eyes for reconciliation, as Christ did. Loving the "other" is what God's perfection looks like. God's perfection looks like taking the risk to fully present with the "other" while holding the hope of mutual transformation through genuine *I-You-We* encounters. God's networked kingdom is like a life-giving, contagious virus spreading; we can't help but sneeze God's in-breaking good news in small ways that can have big effects and, sometimes, lead to dramatic transformation.

Recommended Resources for Further Reflection

Michael Frost and Alan Hirsch, *The Shaping of Things to Come: Innovation and Mission for the 21st Century Church* (Peabody, MA: Hendrickson, 2003).

Seth Godin, *Unleashing the Ideavirus* (New York: Hyperion, 2001).

Colin Greene and Martin Robinson, *Metavista: Bible, Church and Mission in an Age of Imagination* (Carlisle, UK: Paternoster, 2008).

Christine D. Pohl, *Making Room: Recovering Hospitality as a Christian Tradition* (Grand Rapids: Eerdmans, 1999).

Emanuel Rosen, *The Anatomy of Buzz: How to Create Word-of-Mouth Marketing* (New York: Doubleday, 2002).

Alan Roxburgh and Fred Romanuk, *The Missional Leader: Equipping Your Church to Reach a Changing World* (San Francisco: Jossey-Bass, 2006).

Questions for Personal Reflection or Small Group Conversation

- Missional *And'ing* is about living as an agent in God's mission of reconciliation. What helps you see hope for connection when a relationship has been marked by division? Is reconciliation really possible?
- What do you understand reconciliation to look like in the lives of those walking in the Way of Christ?
- Describe a personal experience of being a "stranger." From your own experience, why is welcoming the stranger so important?
- Recall a time when you initiated a "weak link." Did anything result that you are aware of?

Network Ecology

Caring for the Networks You Are In

To live in this world you must be able to do three things: to love what
is mortal; to hold it against your bones knowing your own life depends
on it; and, when the time comes to let it go, to let it go.[1]

Mary Oliver

Living about a mile and a half from Microsoft's main campus and
just a bit farther down the road from Nintendo, I often run into hi-
tech professionals. When I run into these folks, I like asking them
to describe what they do. In one such recent conversation, a "network engineer" described his responsibilities as "the maintenance
of computer hardware and software that comprises a computer
network." He went on to say that this normally includes "the deploy-
ment, configuration, monitoring, and maintenance of the network
equipment in relationship with their software application and [his
company]'s missional objectives." I listened with great interest as this
young man explained that stewarding the whole computer network
involved far more than making sure everyone had a computer and
that their computers could connect with each other. Rather, his care
of the network called for a deep understanding of how the unique

147

missional needs of his company guide the shape and function of its computer network. This hi-tech professional's emphasis on missional relationship between the hardware and the software got me thinking about how leaders of churches and other organizations monitor and care for the relationship between their hardware—like the institutions, structures, polities, or Christ-Commons (body)—and their software—the Spirit-led Christ-Clusters (soul).

If a church or a Christ-Commons is like hardware in God's networked kingdom, then how are we to wisely steward the hardware and software of our local network? How do our local missional goals give unique purpose and shape to our care for our Christ-Commons? Are pastors and ministry leaders a type of network engineer? What does it mean to steward a network so that the people in our communities are more likely to dynamically cluster together as a blessing to the world?

In this chapter we are going to explore the vital task of network ecology. Ecology is the study and care of living systems, so our focus will be on how to care for the living systems of our life together in local faith communities. How do we care for our local Christ-Commons knowing that they are connected to God's larger network? We will consider what it means for us to participate with God in the stewardship of our local networks so that clustering in Christ is more likely to happen than not.

> Our challenge for the future is that we realize we are very much a part of the earth's ecosystem, and we must learn to respect and live according to the basic biological laws of nature.[2]
>
> Jim Fowler

Learning from Other Living Systems

As we consider what it means for us to care for our living networks, it seems wise to turn our attention to other living systems and let them be our teachers. With the life of our living Christ-Commons in mind, I'd like to turn our attention to the field of ecology. Throughout the pages of Scripture, we see the biblical writers using the life sciences to illustrate or teach living in the way of Jesus. Often in Proverbs we're nudged toward wisdom by watching ants, deer, or birds, or by learning to read the signs of the wind, clouds, or rain.[3] Other times we're guided to reflect on leadership by listening to a lion's roar or watching the dew on the grass. "Reaping and sowing" is a recurring metaphor in Scripture, as is respecting the seasons of the year or seasons of life.

Jesus frequently invited his listeners to learn from observing the natural world. We already considered his use of yeast and mustard seeds. Jesus also spoke of the gift of pruning; about vineyards and the flow of life from the vine to the branches; about wheat and weeds growing together. He invites us to reflect on what the splendor of the birds and the lilies of the fields might suggest about our God-given worth, and offers numerous other life lessons from nature. In this tradition, we now turn our attention to ecology.

Ecology is a focused study of learning how living systems work, so it holds tremendous insights for caring for our families, churches, and even our personal lives. Throughout *Thy Kingdom Connected*, we've seen that everything and everyone is interconnected. From the vantage point of interconnectedness, we understand life to be an ecosystem, meaning that what happens to one or to a cluster has ripple-like effects for all. Given God's networked ecokingdom, the question before us is: How do we steward our lives and our communities such that abundant life flourishes not just for you and me but for everyone and everything? Our hope should be to build and steward sustainable communities in which we can satisfy our needs and aspirations without diminishing the same for future generations.

Ecosystems can teach us much about living sustainably. Sustainability is a characteristic of a process or state that can be maintained at a certain level indefinitely. For our purposes, sustainability will not focus on the individual person, nor on the local Christ-Commons, but the sustainability and vitality of the networked kingdom of God. Ecosystems are paradoxically both opened and closed systems of interconnection. As we look at both openness and closedness, we will see that both are vital for our churches, and that failure to hold both in tension will cause not only our churches to suffer but the world as well. Let's begin by looking at closed ecosystems.

Ecosystems Are Differentiated Networks

An ecosystem consists of a closed pattern of nodes relating to each other; every ecosystem is a *We* identity. Through their pattern of relating with each other, the nodes within an ecosystem create a boundary around it. This self-created boundary is important to differentiate one ecosystem from other ecosystems. In a cell this closed boundary is a thin membrane. Inside the membrane we find the DNA and RNA giving the cell its unique identity. In a church, that closed boundary may be its membership rolls; in a car club the boundary might be owning a VW Beetle. A closed system is called an *autopoiesis*, a rather technical-sounding word that simply means "self-created." It's the idea that community has to give some definition as to what it means to belong to a given community.

More specifically, autopoiesis, a concept developed by Chilean biologists Humberto Maturana and Francisco Varela, expresses the dialectical relationship of form (or structure) and function in living systems. Louis Sullivan, the famous American architect credited as the father of modern architecture and the skyscraper, famously said that "form follows function." While form may follow function when designing a building, after the building is constructed, the building's form dictates the functions; any church with an older building knows this to be true. In living systems form and function dance together, allowing for adaptive changes in response to changing contexts, resources, personalities, and gifts. This ongoing dance creates the dynamic identity of the ecosystem. The forms of your church may include your denomination, polity, building, and the like, while your functions include things like your worship, discipleship, teaching, Eucharist, and social gatherings. And your forms and functions dance together to shape your church's unique identity. This is a closed ecosystem; your local community is not the same as the church down the road.

Any identifiable network to which you belong is a closed ecosystem. That might sound off-putting and a bit exclusionary, but hear me out. To have an identity as a network, a network must be able to define itself, and self-knowledge is essential for any kind of relationship. Just as I must have an "*I*" identity in order to offer myself to "*You*" in a genuine *I & You* encounter, so a network must understand itself as having a unique identity for the sake of relationship. That is what we mean by saying that an ecosystem is closed; an ecosystem has a self-created, differentiated identity. It is an autopoietic system; its self-created identity is its dance of form and function in its own unique context.

Furthermore, each ecosystem has a distinctive identity that is constantly reproduced in its communication, and depends on what is considered meaningful and what is not. If an ecosystem fails to maintain that identity, it ceases to exist as a system and dissolves back into the environment from which it emerged. Churches, too, must constantly reproduce themselves through the telling of God's story in their contexts and enacting the drama of baptism, communion, discipleship, and the various missional communication that forms our unique *We* identity. Failure to maintain this identity would result in the dissolution of a church.

Our *We* identity is forever in the process of being created in and through the stories we tell, the actions we take, and our liturgical practices that give form to our gathering.[4] It is often said that the church is the people, but the study of ecosystems suggest that may not be entirely accurate. The church is people, but it is our shared language, practices, and narratives that actually knit the people together. This slight readjustment in thinking is helpful because it enables us to see the way a social network is unique. Our churches are more than the sum of the people gathered; they are the people gathered in Christ, united in story, ritual, and missional living. If we are wise network ecologists, we will help those in our networks become fluent in communicating and embodying those practices that make up the identity of our network. Again, it must be stressed that as Christians we don't do this as simply a network of people, for our network identity is formed first and foremost by our clustering together in Jesus Christ and by the presence of the Holy Spirit in our specific context. As such the stories we tell and the actions in which we engage are formed in continuity with the revealed story of God in Scripture.

Our little faith networks live into their networked identity not simply as an isolated dance of form and function in their context but also by God's bigger picture as seen throughout Scripture: the picture of *shalom* in the Tanakh, or the kingdom of God as Jesus announced it.

Local churches are localized contextual ecosystems seeking to embody God's now-and-not-yet dream for creation. God's bigger picture is life as God created it to be, and it is the life God is calling forth in the re-creation of all things. Throughout the history of the people of God, form and function have danced together responsively to promote the life of God in an array of contexts—from a leaderless mass of Jacob's enslaved descendants to a mobilized group of freedom riders under Moses's leadership; from a nomadic people whose worship life centered around the Ten Commandments and the tabernacle to a budding nation centered around God's presence in Jerusalem's temple; from a Jewish sect of Jesus followers to a Gentile-inclusive movement of Christianity. All of these changes in the people of God reveal the autopoietic nature of form and function as the living system of God's people sought to live faithfully in their contexts. We could go on to look at changes like the Roman merger of church and state and the Protestant Reformation: more than theological shifts, these are all examples of the dance of form and function, the living ecosystem of God's kingdom adapting to contextual shifts.

Wise pastors and ministry leaders will steward their networks by helping the people in their ecosystem live the stories and practices that form the *We* of their life together. Wise pastors and ministry leaders will help form a close, differentiated community that is unique from other communities (lest it cease to be a community at all). This is why it is so important for pastors to be "conservative," for we are conserving that which gives us our unique identity. Please don't stop reading here, because there is a vital tension to be held: wise leaders must simultaneously foster open structures also.

Ecosystems Are Open Structures

Ecosystems are not only closed organizations with unique identities; they are also open structures. As we've seen time and again throughout this project, the relational vision of God's networked kingdom often holds together what at first glance can appear to be opposing realities. Ecosystems are simultaneously closed and open systems. They are organizationally closed while structurally open. What does this mean for you and me?

Well, for starters this means that as we lead our communities, we help them form a secure identity as people of God in such a way that they can be freed to open themselves up to new contexts, relationships, cultures, and experiences without fearing their *We* identity is forfeited. Admittedly, this is complex. Genuine openness means that the *We* identity will be shaped and altered by open encounters with the other. If we understood this solely as a human endeavor, I would say it may be impossible, but the church is Christ's church and the Holy Spirit is active in calling the church forward as a bride prepares for her bridegroom. So it is with the knowledge that God is already and always at work in God's people that we steward these little networks to live into the dance of openness and closedness with humility and conviction, with grace and curiosity, and with great courage as we boldly link where no one has linked before.

We already learned the technical term for a closed organization is *autopoietic*. The technical term used for open structures is *dissipative*. A dissipative structure is characterized by the spontaneous appearance of symmetry breaking and the formation of complex, sometimes chaotic, structures where interacting particles exhibit long-range correlations. (Wow, that was a mouthful.) Have you ever been at an annual church meeting where, out of the blue, a comment was made that disrupted everything? That's dissipative, and it is vital for the life of your community. Usually such seemingly "out of the blue" comments are a challenge to either the form or the function of your community. And though it is almost always difficult to navigate such disruption, it can be embraced as an invitation to life. This really is one of the fascinating tensions of living systems and part of what makes stewarding a faith community so exciting. How do we foster the ecosystem of our faith communities so that they are organizationally closed, thus creating a *We* identity, while ensuring that they are structurally open so they are being transformed through encountering other people, ideas, cultures, and experiences? To ask this question even more simply: What does it mean to be in the world and not of the world? This is at the heart of stewarding a Christ-Commons in God's networked kingdom.

Failing to hold this tension well has disastrous consequences. And frankly, human beings have a poor track record of holding this tension well. This is why I want us to lean into this somewhat heady conversation. The wisdom literature of Scripture and the teachings of Jesus keep calling us back to the thoughtful study of the created order, especially living systems. Throughout history we have revealed a tendency to think that if someone or another group is not part of our *We*, then we must conquer them before they conquer us; we must ignore them before they can ignore us; or we must surrender our missional identity, choosing not to engage and, in consequence, we begin to turn in on ourselves. This may be part of what Jesus was inviting in his call to love our enemies and pray for those who persecute us.

When a person is overcome by fear, feeling that others are "out to get them," the person has a very difficult time opening themselves in relationship with others. But when a person's sense of self is relatively intact, then opening to others is possible. Here's the challenge: as soon as a person opens him- or herself up to encountering another, the person moves out of equilibrium. A genuine encounter with another always opens a person up to change. It is the dance of order with chaos; it is the abundant life Christ talked about.

Transformation through Relationship

As your church community opens itself up to encounter those things, people, or resources that are outside of its network, your community moves into a state of nonequilibrium, and nonequlibirum causes change. Equilibrium is the condition of a system in which competing influences are balanced. Nonequlibirum is not simply being out of balance; rather, it is a state in which a system experiences irreversible transformations. When an animal species goes extinct, for example, its ecosystem is thrown into a state of irreversible transformation until a new and different equilibrium emerges.

Phyllis Tickle's book *The Great Emergence* walks through the church's history and current experience of being thrown into a state of nonequilibrium that appears to be setting the stage for an irreversible transformation.[5] Like the Great Reformation (roughly five hundred years ago), and the Great Schism (roughly one thousand years ago), and the Great Transition (roughly fifteen hundred years ago), the church's current transformation will transform the face of Christianity. For those of us who love Christ's church, putting "church" and "irreversible transformation" in the same sentence can sound frightening. Surely prayerful wisdom is required now as much as any time in history. Do we believe that God is present and active with us in forming Christ's church? Can God be trusted to nudge us toward fullness of life?

Transformation literally means going beyond your form.[6]

Wayne Dyer

Thriving in Nonequilibrium

Because most ecosystems regularly encounter foreign things, people, and resources, they function in a state of nonequilibrium. Living ecosystems are not only able to maintain their life process under conditions of nonequilibrium, but they actually thrive in this state. Often the introduction of foreign bodies into an ecosystem gives the ecosystem the opportunity to enact its unique form-and-function dance while modulating for the slight change in context.

Lynette and I have lived in the Seattle area for about thirteen years. Ten of these years we have intentionally shared our home with other people. Although we didn't start off with this intention, we have discovered that the introduction of another person in addition to our immediate family provides an opportunity for our family to enact our unique dance of form and function. We have consistently found that sharing our home invites us to see ourselves and change our patterns of being in life-giving ways. Over the years my brother, different people from our faith community, and students have lived with us. Our current housemate is a Muslim man from Tunisia who is working on his MBA. Each housemate we have welcomed into our home has shaped us and altered our family's way of being—from having to adjust to each others' comings and goings from the house, to being exposed to different religious beliefs and practices, to simple things like the smells of the food we cook or adjusting the volume on our TVs and stereos. And this has been a good and beautiful thing; it reminds us that we are not the center of the universe while also presenting the possibility of transformation through relational encounter. This is not to say that it's always been easy or fun, for to welcome another is to invite disequilibrium.

> A diverse ecosystem will also be resilient, because it contains many species with overlapping ecological functions that can partially replace one another. When a particular species is destroyed by a severe disturbance so that a link in the network is broken, a diverse community will be able to survive and reorganize itself. . . . In other words, the more complex the network is, the more complex its pattern of interconnections, the more resilient it will be.[7]

> Fritjof Capra

Closedness and Openness

Thriving life for our communities is the dance of closedness and openness. Of course, this means that our churches and our other networks exist in a constant state of becoming. They are ecosystems in process. Our churches change, respond, and adapt to their morphing culture(s) and context(s). So how do we know how we're doing? Are we stewarding our little ecosystems well? Are we wisely forming a closed *We* identity while simultaneously fostering a genuine openness? How do we gauge the relative health of an ecosystem?

It is very difficult, maybe impossible, to determine a network's relative health by looking at a smaller set within the ecosystem. It's best to look at a larger set. Similarly, it's difficult to gauge the health of a church by looking at one person within the church; or to gauge the health of a denomination by looking at one church; or to gauge the health of the global economy by looking at one country's economy. Biophysicist Robert Rosen puts it this way: "The essence of an open system is . . . the necessity to invoke an 'outside,' or an environment, in order to understand what is going on 'inside.' That is, we must go to a larger system, and not to smaller ones, to account for what an open system is doing."[8] The larger set we use to gauge the relative health of our Christ-Commons is God's networked kingdom. God's capacious narrative as seen throughout Scripture is the narrative that forever envelops our little ecosystems; God's great story animates the forms and functions of our little ecosystems. To determine how your church is doing, don't gauge it by the individuals in your church, or even in comparison to what other churches are doing; go to God's bigger narrative. How is your local faith community participating with God in God's dream for the re-creation of heaven and earth? How is your church participating in the flourishing of God's dream of abundant life for all?

Embracing the Whole Life Cycle

Ecosystems in creation offer an interesting perspective on death. An ecosystem is able to embrace the death of an individual organism as part of the natural lifecycle of all organisms within the ecosystem. Through the death of one organism, other organisms find life. As an animal dies and its body surrenders to the process of decay, it gives life to bacteria, insects, and other animals, and it reintroduces nutrients to the earth. Today it is generally accepted that wildfires are a natural part of a wooded ecosystem. We now know that some plants survive fires by a variety of strategies, or even encourage fire (for example, eucalyptus trees contain flammable oils in their leaves) as a way of eliminating competition from less fire-tolerant species. Smoke, charred wood, and heat are common fire cues that stimulate the germination of seeds. Forest fires are one of the ways forests are revitalized.

Ecosystems see death as an important part of the cycle of life. This holds great hope for us as we are witnessing the decline of many institutional churches and denominations in the Western world. Local churches, and even denominations, are not the totality of God's net-worked kingdom. Churches are like organisms in the larger ecosystem of God's kingdom. As such the "death," or closure, of a church—while to be mourned—is never the last word; for we do not mourn as people without hope. The death of one local network may in fact release kingdom nutrients that allow for new life to blossom.

In any network, one of the ways to invigorate new clustering activity is to remove a cluster hub. When a hub is removed from its central connective role to the nodes connected to it, those nodes will naturally cluster around a new hub. Such clustering activity serves to spur new life, new clusters, and greater interconnectedness. Local church closure is not a death blow to God's networked kingdom. Perfect balance is a death blow to living systems. Fish can't live in a stagnant pond. Periodic oscillations help living systems to thrive. Sometimes a forest fire is just what the forest needs.

In your life and ministry, where have you experienced death? Have there been seasons where the very essence of what you understood to be your calling and mission seemed to be going up in smoke? I don't want to be glib in any way about the reality of pain and suffering in such seasons—we all know that fires, whether literal forest fires or the figurative fires that burn through our faith communities, are painful and cause great short-term damage. But ecosystems reflect something we know about God through Scripture: death does not win.

> The call of death is a call of love. Death can be sweet if we answer it in the affirmative, if we accept it as one of the great eternal forms of life and transformation.[9]
>
> Hermann Hesse

Resurrection and the Transformation of All

Theologian Karl Rahner emphasized that the resurrection of Jesus Christ signals the deepest kind of change within all things in the universe. Rahner called this an ontological change, or a change at the level of *being*. He articulates Christ's death and resurrection as two distinct sides of one event.[10] As ecotheologian Denis Edwards writes, "In death, Jesus freely hands his bodily existence into the mystery of a loving God. In resurrection, God adopts creaturely reality as God's own reality. Jesus in his humanity and as a part of the creaturely world is forever taken into God. God's self-bestowal to the world in the incarnation reaches its culmination in the resurrection, when God divinizes and transfigures the creaturely reality of Jesus."[11] What this means is that the resurrection of Jesus is an event that transforms the whole of creation: you and me, our networks and ecosystems, all the earth and the entire universe. Rahner said that Jesus's incarnation, death, and resurrection—as part of the ecosystem of the physical, biological, and human world—are "the embryonically final beginning of the glorification and divination of the whole of reality."[12]

God becomes part of creation so that creation can find its completeness in God. Death is not our enemy. Even the closure of a church or an entire denomination is not our enemy; in God's networked kingdom new life is born in such things. God, knowing our propensity for such myopic vision, entered this world and transformed it, not only in the presence of Jesus but also in his death and resurrection. God, in infinite wisdom, gives the responsibility of stewarding creation to creation. Now is the time to embrace our God-given privilege and responsibility as network ecologists and steward our communities unto life while mourning, yet not fearing, death. Now is the time to learn from living systems what sustainable kingdom life looks like.

> Christianity is not a theory or speculation, but a life; not a philosophy of life, but a life and a living process.[13]
>
> Samuel Taylor Coleridge

Recommended Resources for Further Reflection

Neil Cole, *Organic Church: Growing Faith Where Life Happens* (San Francisco: Jossey-Bass, 2005).

Denis Edwards, *Ecology at the Heart of Faith* (Maryknoll, NY: Orbis Books, 2006).

Joseph R. Myers, *Organic Community: Creating a Place Where People Naturally Connect* (Grand Rapids: Baker Books, 2007).

Thom S. Rainer and Eric Geiger, *Simple Church: Returning to God's Process for Making Disciples* (Nashville: B&H Publishing Group, 2006).

Questions for Personal Reflection or Small Group Conversation

- Since you likely already care for one or more networks, what did you find helpful about this reading?
- Sometimes our faith communities struggle to hold the tension of being simultaneously closed (differentiated identity) and

open (truly welcoming of the other). Which best reflects your community?

1. We hold the closed/open tension well
2. We have a fairly strong sense of identity but we are not always as open as we could be
3. We are quite open but don't have a strong sense of a *We* identity in Christ
4. Other

- We explored the metaphor of network ecology. What other metaphors help you think about stewarding the connective spaces in your life and community?

10

Weaving a Tapestry

Networking Spiritual Formation

> Spiritual maturity or spiritual fulfillment necessarily involves the whole person—body, mind and soul, place, relationships—in connection with the whole of creation throughout the era of time. . . . Spirituality encompasses the whole person in the totality of existence in the world, not some fragment or scrap or incident of a person.[1]
>
> William Stringfellow

I've lived most of my adult life as a pastor and teacher. My primary hope for those I do life with is that we, together, are mutually formed into people of life, as seen in Christ. Of course I want to excel in my professional responsibilities, such as teaching, leading, organizing, and worship leading, but none of these things are the primary reason I do what I do. My aim is nothing less than active participation with God in weaving a kingdom tapestry together with others as our lives—by the presence of God's Spirit—give unique networked expression of God's unfolding narrative.

I made an unexpected connection between spiritual formation and networks thanks to some in-flight reading. I should say that when I travel I often pick up a magazine or two that allow me to dip into disciplines or hobbies that I have little knowledge of. I'm curious what people write in a magazine focused on dental hygiene or kit cars. Right about the time I began reflecting on the relationship of God's connected kingdom and spiritual formation, I happened to pick up a copy of *Creative Knitting*. I have to confess, I had no idea that so much could be written about patterns, stitching, yarn, and the joy of knitting, but as I flipped through and read, the process of spiritual formation seemed to jump off every page. In weaving, the threads are always straight, running parallel either lengthwise (warp threads) or crosswise (weft threads). By contrast, the yarn in knitted fabrics follows a meandering path (a course), forming symmetric loops (also called bights or stitches) symmetrically above and below the mean path of the yarn. These meandering loops can be stretched easily in different directions, which gives knitted fabrics much more elasticity than woven fabrics; depending on the yarn and knitting pattern, knitted garments can stretch as much as 500 percent.

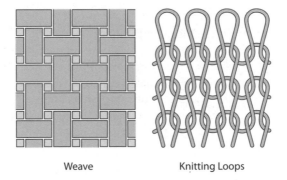

Weave   Knitting Loops

When I later told a friend about the connection I was beginning to see between networks and knitting, he told me about Kevlar. Kevlar is a woven fabric created by DuPont that is used by police and the military in the making of bulletproof vests. Kevlar is five times stronger than steel. It works the way a soccer net stops a ball: the fabric absorbs and disperses the energy and force of an object, such as a bullet or a knife. A unified network of woven threads can absorb and disperse that which threatens its existence.

Tapestries are another form of intricate weavings, of thousands upon thousands of interconnected threads. Each unique thread con-

Centered Set

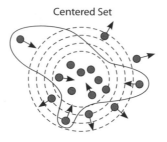

The centered paradigm has some clear advantages for thinking about spiritual formation because it focuses on what is central while allowing for porous boundaries. The centered paradigm helps Christ-followers orient themselves in terms of who God is as revealed in Christ. And the issue is not external boundaries but movement with the Holy Spirit toward Christ. The centered paradigm still maintains a distinction between being a Christian and not being a Christian, but its emphasis is not on maintaining the external boundaries in order to preserve personal purity in order to ensure that one is "in." Rather, the distinction is for the sake of cluster identity. Centered paradigms also allow for and encourage variation among Christians. All are seen as being on different paths along their Christ-centered journeys, and that's a good thing.

Comparing bounded with centered paradigms, Michael Frost and Alan Hirsch give this helpful example:

> Think of the difference between wells and fences. In some farming communities, the farmers might build fences around their properties to keep livestock in and the livestock of neighboring farms out. This is bounded set. But in rural communities where farms cover enormous geographic areas, fencing the property is out of the question. In our home in Australia, ranches (called stations) are so vast that fences are superfluous. Under these conditions a farmer has to sink a bore and create a well, a precious water supply in the Outback. It is assumed that livestock, though they will stray, will never roam too far from the well, lest they die. This is a centered set. As long as there is a clean supply of water, the lives will remain close by.[7]

Hiebert highlights two important dynamics essential for an understanding of networked spiritual formation. First, there is a turning point in a centered paradigm; for example, a person has left another center and made Christ her or his center. Second, there is no static state; one will either continue to move toward or away from the center.

The centered paradigm can help free Christians from rigid fundamentalism while aiding them in focusing on the way of Christ and the networked kingdom. God's networked kingdom conjoins these two paradigms while also linking us to our affective communities so as to further enliven spiritual formation.

Some of the challenges with the centered paradigm concept are that it stresses faithful movement as moving toward the center, with the assumption that the center is a fixed locale. And both paradigms focus more on the individual than on holding the tension of the person in community. I want to suggest a more compressive vision, "the networked paradigm."

> Language about spirituality can be used to separate mind, body and spirit or to separate the spiritual from the political. . . . Dialogue about spirituality tends to be personalistic rather than communal. People seldom address the spiritual health of the community as if it were essential to the spiritual health of the individual.[8]
>
> Lynn N. Rhodes

The "And/Also" of a Networked Paradigm

Both bounded and centered paradigms focus on the individual, and they set up a binary whereby one is either bounded or centered. A networked vision of spiritual formation weaves the best of both the bounded and centered paradigm together in a relational context.

Throughout this book we've seen how networked vision enables us to see more relationally, and even to hold together what we had previously assumed to be opposed. We're about to see that again.

The networked paradigm does not discard the bounded paradigm *carte blanche*. Rather, the networked paradigm takes the seed of truth buried inside the bounded paradigm and frees it to blossom into differentiated beliefs and actions. Differentiated beliefs and actions do not bind the person to a my-way-or-the-highway manner of being; rather, the differentiated person says with deep conviction and openness, "I am here. Where are you?" The differentiating person does not seek to define themselves against others; rather, they offer themselves as honestly and clearly as they can while hoping for an encounter. Every person lives with convictions and beliefs; in fact, convictions and beliefs are essential to life and relationship. Part of what makes you *you*, and me *me*, is that we each have a unique cocktail of convictions, beliefs, and values. Part of the gift of interpersonal relations is offering the fullness of one's unique cocktail of beliefs to those we come in contact with. Of course, this differs from the bounded paradigm in that the networked paradigm does not demand the other to hold convictions and beliefs in the same way as we do. Rather, we humbly present our values to the other knowing that as we move toward a genuine *I & You* encounter, *We* will both be formed, even transformed, by our encounter with the other. But the starting place is in bringing the fullness of yourself (convictions and all) to those you link up with.

The language of Christ-Clusters and Christ-Commons marks one of the most important distinctions between a centered paradigm and networked vision of spiritual formation. The centered paradigm seems to make Christ a goal we are moving toward, while the networked paradigm recognizes that the Holy Spirit is the living presence animating all relationships and is the one who gives form and definition to our Christ-Commons and Christ-Clusters. It is the agency of the Holy Spirit transforming us into the likeness of Christ. In a very real way, networked spiritual formation encourages us to anticipate encountering Christ in the faces of the people we meet throughout the day. And that real presence of Christ through encounter with the other is the encounter in which much of our spiritual formation occurs. God is not some distant goal we journey toward; rather, God is the living presence with whom we journey. I do want to be careful that we don't lose the uniqueness of God. I am not saying that God *is* the other but that we encounter God *through* others. Jesus said:

Then the King will say to those on the right, "Come, you who are blessed by my Father, inherit the Kingdom prepared for you from

169

the foundation of the world. For I was hungry, and you fed me. I was thirsty, and you gave me a drink. I was a stranger, and you invited me into your home. I was naked, and you gave me clothing. I was sick, and you cared for me. I was in prison, and you visited me." Then these righteous ones will reply, "Lord, when did we ever see you hungry and feed you? Or thirsty and give you something to drink? Or a stranger and show you hospitality? Or naked and give you clothing? When did we ever see you sick or in prison, and visit you?" And the King will tell them, "I assure you, when you did it to one of the least of these my brothers and sisters, you were doing it to me!" (Matt. 25:34–40)

The networked paradigm of spiritual formation links you and me together in our formative processes centered in God through Christ by the Holy Spirit as we encounter others; especially as we give voice to the voiceless, welcome the stranger, and care for those who have no one else to care for them. The words of the prophet Micah encapsulate the heart of networked spiritual formation: "O people, the LORD has already told you what is good, and this is what he requires: to do what is right, to love mercy, and to walk humbly with your God" (Mic. 6:8). This vision of spiritual formation links my formation with the well being of others in God's networked kingdom.

Love the animals, love the plants, love everything. If you love everything, you will perceive the divine mystery in things. Once you perceive it, you will begin to comprehend it better every day. And you will come at last to love the whole world with an all-embracing love.[9]

Fyodor Dostoyevsky

Weaving a Tapestry of Spiritual Formation

Weaving a tapestry of spiritual formation invites us to listen for opportunities to help connect the people in our lives to God, to each other, and to the rest of creation in life-promoting ways. In helping others to flourish, our own lives flourish. Any time we gain at the expense of another, we all lose, and any time we find life, all of creation and even God delights, for we are created to know life abundant. Eugene Peterson puts it this way: "Life is the end of life; life, life, and more life. The end of all Christian belief and obedience, witness and teaching, marriage and family, leisure and work life, preaching and pastoral work is the *living* of everything we know about God: life, life, and more life."[10]

Weaving a tapestry of spiritual formation is not about forming dependence on ourselves but helping others find life, connection, and the resources to live as the networked persons God created them to be. It's about active participation in weaving a kingdom tapestry with others as our lives—by the presence of God's Spirit—give unique networked expression to God's unfolding narrative. Sometimes that means helping people move beyond us, which can be difficult for pastors and leaders of organizations. Even more: sometimes what can look like a lack of commitment to a specific church can actually be a dynamic form of kingdom interconnectedness. Consider a woman who works at a law firm with a couple of other Christ-followers. The three have lunch once a week for encouragement and fellowship, to spur one another on toward "love and good deeds" (Heb. 10:24), to nudge each other Christ-ward. She is reading a book by Henri Nouwen, volunteers at a nearby Baptist church's midweek kids' program, and usually attends an Assembly of God service Sunday mornings. Though every once in a while, she opts for Russian Orthodox worship, her official church membership is still at her parents' Lutheran church.

What may look like a fragmented lack of commitment from a bounded paradigm perspective may also be seen as a sign of kingdom connectedness. She is embodying a oneness in Christ that crosses and bridges theological and organizational boundaries. She is clustering with those in her affective communities centered in the person of Christ. She has multiple links knitting her firmly in a kingdom network. In this networked paradigm, the question of her "actual" church membership is blurred. Her spiritual formation is woven into a complex fabric of connections through which her life flourishes while helping others' lives to flourish.

Any thoughtful *And'er* will seek to link other people with other nodes within their cluster. And they will not stop there: *And'ers* will aid each connecting node in weaving a web that safely and uniquely

Peter Senge, Otto Scharmer, Joseph Jaworski, and Betty Sue Flowers, *Presence: Human Purpose and the Field of the Future* (Cambridge, MA: Society for Organizational Learning, 2004).

Questions for Personal Reflection or Small Group Conversation

- Tell the story of your spiritual formation through other people who have influenced your life and journey.
- Which of the three paradigms for imagining spiritual formation (bounded, centered, networked) best reflects your experience? How could you live in a more networked way?
- Describe how you picture your personal and communal life contributing to the tapestry of God's great story.
- What do you think God wants from you and creation? How do you imagine God's dream for you, your community, and the world?

Afterword

The Great Connection

BY DAN B. ALLENDER

My first Christian experience began in a connective community. The college fellowship where I first encountered the living Christ was unaffiliated with any of the large campus ministries. It was a community of young believers who were mentored by a number of older believers from disparate traditions. There was a strong emphasis on the works of the Spirit—tongues, prophesy, and healing. And there was a fascination with Dutch Calvinism, especially Kuyper, and Van Til. Over time our community read Bonheoffer, Schaffer, and the early church fathers.

I didn't do much reading, if any; I was more drawn to the good food, kindness, and sweet women. But I do recall the nature of the discussions, even if I didn't understand their import or controversy. The debate/discussion/dialogue was engaged with vitality, passion, and freedom and when it ended there was prayer and care. I don't recall a single moment where a divergent or discordant view was silenced or met with patronizing instruction, let alone contempt or shame. I didn't encounter that dark experience until I went to seminary.

175

It is common in some circles to bash seminaries. God knows there is something broken in all institutions, let alone people. However, seminary was the first clear environment where it was crucial to divide and separate communities. Whenever you can break groups or communities into acronyms you know you are part of something divisive. We learned there were two communities (isn't it interesting how deeply we love and use polarities?): TRs, who were "truly reformed," and BEs, those who were "broadly evangelical." In that period I wanted to be among the truest and most devoted, and the truly reformed were my ideal. The problem was I continually forgot the specialized words, formulas, and historical antecedents to our truth. I just couldn't remember in which book Calvin spoke about baptism, nor did I care. I was interested in his views, but then I was more interested in the fact that when my favorite professor Ray Dillard spoke of Calvin, his eyes twinkled like he was quoting a friend, not a prooftext that finished an argument.

I gravitated to the humanity of my professors as much if not more than their ideas. It has been one of the theological bedrocks of my evolving theological journey. Listen for truth lived, suffered, and fought, not merely believed. What intrigues me is not so much what you believe (truly, this is obviously important), but what you have fought not to believe yet can't help but confess is true. It is that set of convictions that are the pearls of great price to be pursued.

Does that provide an assurance that one will find both orthopraxy and orthodoxy? Not at all. It is far easier to find one or the other in their division. I find many orthodox I couldn't bear spending an hour with let alone going to a pub to drink a beer. I find many heterodox infinitely more human, kind, and curious, yet unwilling or unable to enter realms of gratitude for a Savior who is, in my estimation, the true essence of being human.

To find orthodoxy and orthopraxy in fluidity of development—broken, messy, inconsistent, yet moving toward a compelling beauty—I have had to look to Dwight. Of course, there must be countless others who embody his passion for both life that is true and truth that brings life, but I have found few who do so as radically or as well. He is passionate to confess Jesus is the truth, way, and the life, but he is unwilling to presume his way of knowing Jesus is the *only* way, truth, and life.

What is required to live a connective life? A connective life requires fierce humility that doesn't canonize one's convictions, yet offers to others the convictions that are precious to our way of living. A connective life calls us to seize all ground of commonality in dialogue or debate with joy rather than reluctance. And it requires an imagination embodied through countless discussions with people from around the world, every race, tongue, and people group, to gainsay the rich complexity of how the gospel is conceived and birthed as the local manifestation of God's universal truth. Humility, joy, and imagination are for me the fruit of the death, resurrection, and ascension of Jesus. All connective theology begins with the core reality of the story of Jesus. The center of our life together is the conviction that Jesus uniquely and solely brings redemption found in no other person, system, or way. Yet all other persons, systems, and ways can't help but illumine the necessity and fundamental glory of the way of Jesus.

To put it another way: all good stories, ultimately, are about the gospel—the great connection. If the gospel of Jesus's life, death, resurrection, and ascension is the story that illumines and captures all other stories before his feet, then why do we fear other stories? Why do we refuse to tell other stories? Why do we refuse to be broken and transformed by other stories since every good story is about suffering (death), reconciliation (resurrection), and the just use of power (ascension). If our core is solid, then why not open our doors to receive into our midst the radical diversity of stories and people that will compel us to see the work of Jesus with new eyes?

A connective life demands far more maturity than I currently enjoy. As I age, the sinews of my body seem stiffer and the weariness of my soul greater. Perhaps a connective life is for the young and the adventurous. Or maybe I need to humble myself to ask the Spirit to help me address the fear of the messiness and impurity of addition. And then ask the Spirit to give me courage to imagine how the disparate and contradictory may be angles of repose that invite me to a new way of seeing. And then maybe, just maybe, I might be the new creation I was meant to be.

Notes

Preface

1. Václav Havel, "The New Measure of Man," *New York Times*, July 8, 1994.

2. Dietrich Bonhoeffer, *Life Together: A Discussion of Christian Fellowship*, trans. John W. Doberstein (New York: Harper and Row, 1954).

3. David Bohm as quoted by Joseph Jaworski in *Synchronicity: The Inner Path of Leadership* (San Francisco: Berrett-Koehler, 1996), 172.

4. Henry David Thoreau, *The Thoughts of Thoreau*, ed. Edwin Way Teale (New York: Dodd, Mead, 1962), 231.

Introduction

1. Marcel Proust, *The Captive, The Fugitive,* and *Time Regained*, vol. 3, *Remembrance of Things Past*, trans. Scott Moncrief (New York: Vintage, 1982), 260.

2. Fritjof Capra, *The Web of Life: A New Scientific Understanding of Living Systems* (New York: Anchor Books, 1996), 4.

3. There are many books that explore these shifts. Two I recommend are Phyllis Tickle, *The Great Emergence: How Christianity Is Changing and Why* (Grand Rapids: Baker Books, 2008) and Leonard Sweet, *Soul Tsunami: Sink or Swim in the New Millennium Culture* (Grand Rapids: Zondervan, 1999).

4. Barbara Reynolds, ed., *The Letters of Dorothy L. Sayers 1937–1943: From Novelist to Playwright* (New York: St Martin's Press, 1998), 158.

5. Thomas S. Kuhn, *The Structure of Scientific Revolutions*, 2nd ed. (Chicago: University of Chicago Press, 1970), 175.

6. Albert Einstein, as quoted by Fritjof Capra, *The Tao of Physics* (Boston: Shambhala Publications, 1991), 331.

7. By "avant-church" I am referring to the cluster of ecclesial expressions exploring what it means to faithfully follow Christ in the new paradigm. The term *avant-garde* has historically been used to describe movements of experimentation

with "new" concepts in politics and art. The term was first used by Napoleon's army to describe an elite force that would stealthily get behind enemy lines to gather information to better prepare the rest of the army for encountering their enemy.

8. The term "the other" can be a highly flexible term. I will be using it in a broad sense to refer to anyone one other than the self. As such, it can include both other people and God.

9. Leo Tolstoy, *What Men Live By* (Mount Vernon, NY: The Peter Pauper Press, 1965), 56–58.

10. Margaret J. Wheatley and Myron Kellner-Roger, *A Simpler Way* (San Francisco: Berrett-Koehler, 1999), 140.

11. Cornelius Plantinga Jr., *Not the Way It's Supposed to Be: A Breviary of Sin* (Grand Rapids: Eerdmans, 1995), 10.

12. Friedrich Nietzsche, *Thus Spake Zarathustra: A Book for All and None*, trans. Thomas Common (Radford, VA: Wilder Publications, 2008), 24.

13. Erich Jantsch, *The Self-Organizing Universe* (Oxford: Pergamon, 1980), 196.

Chapter One: The Networked Kingdom

1. Catherine Keller, *From a Broken Web* (Boston: Beacon Press, 1986), 159.

2. Duncan Watts, *Small World: The Dynamics of Networks between Order and Randomness* (Princeton: Princeton University Press, 2003).

3. Albert-László Barabási and Eric Bonabeau, "Scale-Free Networks," *Scientific American*, May 2003, 54.

4. Frederic B. Burnham, "A Natural Theology of Community: Network Theory and Church Leadership," unpublished manuscript, 2006, 8.

5. Ibid., 10.

6. Oliver O'Donovan, as quoted by Jeremy S. Begbie, *Voicing Creation's Praise: Towards a Theology of the Arts* (Edinburgh: T&T Clark International, 2000), 205.

7. These words are my paraphrasing of numerous passages in the Gospels, including Matthew 12:28, Luke 4:18, and Luke 15.

8. S. Jonathan Bass, *Blessed Are the Peacemakers: Martin Luther King Jr., Eight White Religious Leaders, and the "Letter from Birmingham Jail"* (Baton Rouge, LA: Louisiana State University Press, 2001), 239.

9. Hawoong Jeong and his colleagues at the University of Notre Dame generated this map. http://www.sciam.com/2001/0801issue/0801scicit7.html, http://fig.cox.miami.edu/~cmallery/150/gene/proteomics.htm.

10. Craig S. Keener, *A Commentary on the Gospel of Matthew* (Grand Rapids: Eerdmans, 1999), 387–88.

11. Mark Buchanan, *Ubiquity: Why Catastrophes Happen* (New York: Three Rivers Press, 2002), 175.

12. Eberhard Jüngel, *God's Being Is in Becoming: The Trinitarian Being of God in the Theology of Karl Barth*, trans. John Webster (Grand Rapids: Eerdmans, 2001), 78.

Chapter Two: Links

1. Coretta Scott King, *The Words of Martin Luther King Jr.* (New York: Newmarket Press, 1987), 3.

2. Shane Hipps, *The Hidden Power of Electronic Culture: How Media Shapes Faith, the Gospel, and Church* (Grand Rapids: Zondervan, 2005), 95–96.

3. Fritjof Capra, *The Web of Life: A New Scientific Understanding of Living Systems* (New York: Anchor Books, 1996), 17.

4. Rupert Sheldrake, as quoted in Peter Senge, C. Otto Scarmer, Joseph Jaworski, and Betty Sue Flowers, *Presence: An Exploration of Profound Change in People, Organizations, and Society* (Cambridge, MA: Society for Organizational Learning, 2004), 207.

5. Margaret J. Wheatley and Myron Kellner-Roger, *A Simpler Way* (San Francisco: Berrett-Koehler, 1999), 140.

6. People can and do have a relationship with themselves, often referred to as intrapsychic relationships. Though some are beginning to explore the idea of relating to oneself, which generally has more to do with understanding one's own story than self-concepts, that understanding of intrapsychic relationship is outside the scope of this project.

7. Iconographers describe their work as "writing," rather than painting, to stress the theological orientation of their work. The word *iconography* literally means "image writing."

8. Michael Lawler writes, "The root meaning of *perichoresis* is seen best in the verb from which it derives, *perichorein*. According to Liddell and Scott, *chorein* means to make room for another, *peri* means round about. *Perichoresis* is the noun, naming the dynamic process of making room for another around oneself." In what Lawler regards "as a fortuitous error, theologically, Robert Kress mistakenly derived *perichoresis* not from *perichorein* but from *perichoreuein*, to dance round. . . . Though *perichorein* and *perichoreuein* are not related etymologically, they are most definitely related in what they connote . . . the three Thous joyfully dance and interweave hand in hand, making room for one another in intricate relatedness and communion" (Michael G. Lawler, "Perichoresis: New Theological Wine In an Old Theological Wineskin," *Horizons* 22, no. 1 [1995]: 49, 53).

9. Augustine, *The Trinity*, trans. Edmond Hill, ed. John E. Rotelle (New York: New City Press, 1990). Augustine's articulation of the Holy Spirit as the bond of love between the Father and the Son has come under considerable scrutiny in recent decades, suggesting a diminishing of the personhood of the Holy Spirit; I would suggest we read Augustine's *Trinity* with a more robust understanding of relationships as living beings as I'm proposing throughout this text.

10. Stanley J. Grenz, *Created for Community: Connecting Christian Belief with Christian Living* (Grand Rapids: Baker Books, 1996), 47.

Chapter Three: Nodes

1. John Wheeler, as quoted by Diarmuid O'Murchu, *Quantum Theology: Spiritual Implications of the New Physics* (New York: Crossroad Publishing, 2004), 3.

2. Michel Foucault, *The Archaeology of Knowledge and the Discourse on Language* (New York: Harper Torchbooks, 1972), 211.

3. Martin Luther King Jr. (1963), as cited on the U.S. Department of State's International Programs website (http://usinfo.state.gov/products/pubs/civilrts/excerpts.htm).

4. Frederick Buechner, *Listening to Your Life: Daily Meditations with Frederick Buechner* (New York: HarperOne, 1992), 139–40.

5. Barack Obama, *The Audacity of Hope: Thoughts on Reclaiming the American Dream* (New York: Crown Publishers, 2008), 1–2.

6. Sallie McFague, *A New Climate for Theology: God, the World, and Global Warming* (Minneapolis: Fortress Press, 2008), 29.

7. Peter Senge, *The Fifth Discipline: The Art and Practice of the Learning Organization* (New York: Doubleday, 1990), 68–69.

8. The Dalai Lama, in a March 1997 speech marking the thirty-eighth anniversary of the Tibetan National Uprising Day.

9. Chief Seattle as cited in Al Gore, *Earth in the Balance: Ecology and the Human Spirit* (Rodale Books, 2006), 259.

10. Jeffrey Sachs, "Weapons of Mass Salvation," *The Economist*, October 24, 2002.

11. John Muir, as quoted by W. Noel Keyes, *Bioethical and Evolutionary Approaches to Medicine and the Law* (Chicago: American Bar Association, 2007), 6.

12. George Bernard Shaw, *Pygmalion* (Sioux Falls, SD: NuVision Publications, 2008), 91

13. Walter Truett Anderson, *The Future of the Self: Inventing the Postmodern Person* (New York: Jeremy P. Tarcher/Putnam, 1997), xi.

14. Veronica Zundel, ed., *Eerdmans Book of Famous Prayers* (Grand Rapids: Eerdmans, 1983), 30.

Chapter Four: Connective Leaders

1. Jean Lipman-Blumen, *Connective Leadership: Managing in a Changing World* (Oxford: Oxford University Press, 1996), 339.

2. It is important to highlight the risk of hubbing in human relationships. Some nodes will attach themselves to a hub solely for the links available through the hub. Because of our understanding of the social self, when any node seeks self and the self's fulfillment, the health of the entire ethos is jeopardized. This is why it is essential for every node to own their relative hubbing role, and their inescapable influence in shaping the communal ethos. When nodes seek self, the ethos of the cluster becomes increasingly self-seeking; conversely, when nodes seek the fulfillment of the other, the ethos becomes increasingly marked by love. "Networking" or "working the room" is using relationships for selfish gain.

3. Max DePree, *Leadership Is an Art* (New York: Dell, 1989), 28.

4. Thomas F. Torrance, *The Christian Doctrine of God: One Being, Three Persons* (Edinburgh: T&T Clark, 1996), 246.

5. Christ's hypostatic union even finds visible expression in the physicality of the cross: with one vertical beam (God to humanity) and one horizontal beam (human to human). The fact that Christ bridges between one repentant thief and one unrepentant thief may further bear witness to the bridging of Christ as the mission of God.

6. These links can be to the other concurrent clusters that share similar characteristics or the links could be to denominations, or learning institutions, or a great cloud of witnesses—past and present—through their writings, websites, other forms of media, etc.

7. Left to themselves, rogue clusters turn into viruses within the network as a whole. The nodes making up these rogue clusters continue to live and relate, and their influence spreads throughout their nodal networks. And the longer those groups are left without healthy interaction with nodes from outside the rogue cluster, the more pervasive the ethos of the rogue community becomes.

8. David E. Bjork, *Unfamiliar Paths: The Challenge of Recognizing the Work of Christ in Strange Clothing* (Pasadena, CA: William Carey Library, 1997), 65.

9. For further treatment of leadership as influence, see Gary A. Yukl, *Leadership in Organizations* (Englewood Cliffs, NJ: Prentice-Hall, 1981), 3; Paul Hersey and Kenneth H. Blanchard, *Management of Organizational Behavior* (Englewood Cliffs, NJ: Prentice-Hall, 1988), 5; John C. Maxwell, *Developing the Leader within You* (Nashville: Thomas Nelson, 1993), 1; Howard Gardner, *Leading Minds* (New York: Basic Books, 1996), 8–9; and Walter C. Wright, *Relational Leadership: A Biblical Model for Leadership Service* (Carlisle, UK: Paternoster, 2000), 23–62.

10. J. Oswald Sanders, *Spiritual Leadership*, rev. ed. (Chicago: Moody, 1980), 35.

11. Leonard I. Sweet, *Summoned to Lead* (Grand Rapids: Zondervan, 2004).

12. Alistair Iain McFadyen, *The Call to Personhood: A Christian Theory of the Individual in Social Relationships* (Cambridge: Cambridge University Press, 1990), 116.

13. Peter Senge, *The Fifth Discipline: The Art and Practice of the Learning Organization* (New York: Doubleday, 1990), 340.

14. Conrad Gempf, *Jesus Asked: What He Wanted to Know* (Grand Rapids: Zondervan, 2003).

15. Jürgen Moltmann, *The Power of the Powerless: The Word of Liberation for Today*, trans. Margaret Kohl (San Francisco: Harper & Row, 1983).

Chapter Five: Leading Connectively

1. Margaret J. Wheatley, *Leadership and the New Science: Discovering Order in a Chaotic World* (San Francisco: Berrett-Koehler, 1999), 34.

2. The summary comment from Morris in his commentary on John 10:10. Leon Morris, *The Gospel according to John*, NICNT (Grand Rapids: Wm. B. Eerdmans, 1971), 509.

3. Anaïs Nin, *Anaïs Nin Reader*, edited by Philip K. Jason (Athens, OH: The Swallow Press, 1975), 260.

4. Erwin Schrödinger, *What Is Life? The Physical Aspect of the Living Cell* (New York: Macmillan & Co., 1945). The book contains a discussion of negentropy and the concept of a complex molecule with the genetic code for living organisms; it was this book that inspired James Watson's further study of the gene, leading to the discovery of the DNA double helix structure. Schrödinger may well be most famous for the paradoxical "Schrödinger's Cat Thought Experiment."

5. Carl Gustauv Jung, as cited by Mary Menke, *The Light at the End of the Tunnel: Coming Back to Life After a Spouse Dies* (Bloomington, IN: AuthorHouse, 2006), 23.

6. The Greek word Χάος, from which we get "chaos," refers to "primal emptiness" or "space."

7. B. B. Mandelbrot, *The Fractal Geometry of Nature* (New York: W. H. Freeman, 1982).

8. Dee W. Hock, *Birth of the Chaordic Age* (San Francisco: Berrett-Koehler, 2000).

9. The dynamical system concept is a mathematical formalization for any fixed "rule" that describes the time dependence of a point's position in its ambient space.

10. Margaret Wheatley, *Finding Our Way: Leadership for an Uncertain Time* (San Francisco: Barrett-Koehler, 2005), 4, 28.

11. Sally Morgenthaler, "Leadership in a Flattened World: Grassroots Culture and the Demise of the CEO Model," in *An Emergent Manifesto of Hope*, ed. Doug Pagitt and Tony Jones (Grand Rapids: Baker Books, 2007), 188.

12. Carl Zimmer, "Scientist at Work: Martin Nowak," *New York Times*, July 31, 2007.

13. Max DePree, *Leadership Is an Art* (New York: Dell, 1989), 3.

Chapter Six: Christ-Commons

1. Senge et al., *Presence*, 7.

2. These two chapters are not designed to form an ecclesiology, but rather a network lens through which we can relationally reimagine how our respective ecclesiologies participate with God in God's already-and-not-yet kingdom.

3. Christ-Commons or institutions begin as dynamic Christ-Clusters. When clusters that dynamically connect around a hub decide to intentionally gather, establishing a regular pattern to their collective existence, the cluster begins the social process of group reification. This group process forms the basis to develop a Christ-Commons and over time to develop its own traditions.

4. Elie Wiesel, *US News & World Report*, October 27, 1986.

5. Sharon Daloz Parks in a talk at a faculty retreat with Mars Hill Graduate School, 2007.

6. Jeff Cook is a personal friend pastoring in Winnipeg, Manitoba. This quotation comes from personal correspondence.

7. Michael Jinkins, *The Church Faces Death: Ecclesiology in a Post-Modern Context* (New York: Oxford University Press, 1999), 102.

Chapter Seven: Christ-Clusters

1. Albert Einstein, as cited by Richard Dawkins, *The Selfish Gene*, 30th anniv. ed. (New York: Oxford University Press, 2006), 329.

2. William S. Beck, *Modern Science and the Nature of Life* (New York: Harcourt, Brace & Co., 1957), 100.

3. Henry Blackaby, Richard Blackaby, and Claude King, *Experiencing God: Knowing and Doing the Will of God* (Nashville: Lifeway Christian Resources, 2007).

4. I use the idea of "communication" to signify the process of exchanging information, usually via a common system of symbols. It takes a wide variety of forms, from face-to-face conversation, hand signals, messages sent over global telecommunication networks, etc. The process of communication is what allows us to interact with other people; without it, we would be unable to share knowledge or experiences with anything outside of ourselves. The Latin root word of "communication" is *comunicare*, "to make common."

5. Social constructs are generally understood to be the byproducts, often unintended or unconscious, of countless human choices. When we understand the Holy Spirit as active in and through human relationships, these socially-constructed realities can be seen with fresh Kingdom significance. See Peter L. Berger and Thomas Luckmann, *The Social Construction of Reality: A Treatise in the Sociology of Knowledge* (New York: Anchor Books, 1989).

6. Fritjof Capra, *The Web of Life: A New Scientific Understanding of Living Systems* (New York: Anchor Books, 1996), 158.

7. Albert-László Barabási, *Linked: How Everything is Connected to Everything Else and What It Means for Business, Science, and Everyday Life* (New York: Plume, 2003), 73.

8. Jürgen Moltmann, *Theology of Hope* (Minneapolis: Augsburg Fortress, 1993), 337.

9. Arie de Geus, *The Living Company* (Cambridge, MA: Harvard Business School Press, 2002), 9.

10. W. Edwards Deming, *The New Economics for Industry, Government, Education*, 2nd ed. (Cambridge, MA: The MIT Press, 2000), 50–51.

Chapter Eight: Missional *And'ing*

1. Augustine, *On Christian Doctrine*.

2. Jesus, as quoted in Matthew 19:6 (CJB).

3. I use "affective community" to refer to the networks of people whose lives we touch and are touched by most directly and frequently.

4. Christopher Locke, Rick Levine, Doc Searls, and David Weinberger, *The Cluetrain Manifesto: The End of Business as Usual* (Cambridge, MA: Perseus, 2000), 122–23.

5. Darrell L. Guder, ed., *Missional Church: A Vision for the Sending of the Church in North America* (Grand Rapids: Eerdmans, 1998), 264.

6. Ibid., 265.

7. Any node engaged in missionally linking will be changed. It is this process of being shaped in and through missional relationships that could offer fresh understandings of syncretism, contextualization, and incarnational ministry. "If it is possible for personal identities to be transformed by their incorporation into new relationships and patterns of co-intention, then past relations cannot be determinative of identity in a complete, absolute and mechanistic sense" (McFadyen, *Call to Personhood*, 115).

8. Sarah Bernhardt as quoted by Martin Manser, *The New Book of Business Quotations* (London: Lawpack Publishing, 2007), 30.

9. Mark Granovetter, "The Strength of Weak Ties," *American Journal of Sociology* 78 (1973): 1360–80.

10. Though outside the scope of this chapter, the strength of weak links and their social bridging could have far-reaching implications for missions, and could benefit from further exploration.

11. Mark Buchanan, *Nexus: Small Worlds and the Groundbreaking Science of Networks* (New York: W. W. Norton & Company, 2002), 44.

12. Howard A. Snyder, *Kingdom, Church, and World: Biblical Themes for Today* (Eugene, OR: Wipf and Stock, 1985).

13. Buchanan, *Nexus*, 43.

14. John M. Barry, *The Great Influenza: The Epic Story of the Deadliest Plague in History* (New York: Penguin Books, 2004).

15. http://health.discovery.com/centers/coldsflu/cold_trivia.html, accessed July 25, 2008.

Chapter Nine: Network Ecology

1. Mary Oliver, "In Blackwater Woods," in *American Primitive: Poems* (New York: Little, Brown, 1983).

2. Jim Fowler, host of the television show *Mutual of Omaha's Wild Kingdom*.

3. Proverbs 6, 11–19, 27, 30 are peppered with lessons from creation. Take Proverbs 30 for example: "There are four things on earth that are small but unusually wise: Ants—they aren't strong, but they store up food for the winter. Rock badgers—they aren't powerful, but they make their homes among the rocky cliffs. Locusts—they have no king, but they march like an army in ranks. Lizards—they are easy to catch, but they are even found in kings' palaces" (Proverbs 30:24–28).

4. Niklas Luhmann, *Social Systems*, trans. John Bednarz Jr. and Dirk Baecker (Stanford: Stanford University Press, 1995). Building on Maturana and Varela's concept of systems as autopoietic, the German sociologist and social theorist Niklas Luhmann has taken the ecosystem concept of autopoiesis (self-creation) and translated it to help us understand human societies as self-producing systems of communication.

5. Phyllis Tickle, *The Great Emergence: How Christianity Is Changing and Why* (Grand Rapids: Baker Books, 2008).

6. Wayne W. Dyer, *You'll See It When You Believe It: The Way to Your Personal Transformation* (New York: Harper, 2001), 14. Note I have paraphrased from Dwyer's larger quote, "Now consider the prefix 'trans,' which means 'beyond,' 'above,' or in literal terms, 'over.' When we place that prefix in front of 'form,' we get 'transform.' We now add the suffix 'ation,' which means 'action' or 'result,' and we have the word 'transform.' To me this word means the result or action of *going beyond one's form*."

7. Fritjof Capra, *The Web of Life: A New Scientific Understanding of Living Systems* (New York: Anchor Books, 1996), 303.

8. Robert Rosen, *Essays on Life Itself* (New York: Columbia University Press, 1999), 20.

9. Volker Michels, ed., *Hermann Hesse: A Pictorial Biography* (New York: Farrar, Straus, and Giroux, 1975).

10. Karl Rahner, "Dogmatic Questions on Easter," in *Theological Investigations*, vol. 4 (New York: Seabury, 1966), 126.

11. Denis Edwards, *Ecology at the Heart of Faith: The Change of Heart That Leads to a New Way of Living on Earth* (Maryknoll, NY: Orbis Books, 2006), 87.

12. Karl Rahner, "Resurrection," in *Encyclopedia of Theology: A Concise Sacramentum Mundi* (London: Burns and Oates, 1975), 1142.

13. Samuel T. Coleridge, *Samuel Taylor Coleridge: The Major Works*, ed. H. J. Jackson (Oxford: Oxford University Press, 2009), 670.

Chapter Ten: Weaving a Tapestry

1. William Stringfellow, *Politics of Spirituality* (Eugene, OR: Wipf & Stock Publishers, 2006), 22.

2. Paul G. Hiebert, "Conversion, Culture, and Cognitive Categories," in *Gospel in Context* 4 (October 1978): 24–29, and "Sets and Structures: A Study of Church Patterns," in *New Horizons in World Missions*, ed. David J. Hesselgrave (Grand Rapids: Baker Books, 1979), 217–27.

3. Ibid., 220.

4. Ibid., 221.

5. Martin Buber, *I and Thou* (New York: Charles Scribner's Sons, 1970), 156.

6. Paul G. Hiebert, "Sets and Structures," 223–24.

7. Michael Frost and Alan Hirsch, *The Shaping of Things to Come: Innovation and Mission for the Twenty-first Century Church* (Peabody, MA: Hendrickson, 2003), 47.

8. Lynn N. Rhodes, *Co-creating: A Feminist Vision of Ministry* (Collegville, MN: Liturgical Press, 2004), 45.

9. Fyodor Dostoyevsky, *The Karamazov Brothers*, trans. Constance Black Garnett and A. D. P. Briggs (Hertfordshire, UK: Wordsworth Editions, 2007), 352.

10. Eugene Peterson, *Christ Plays in Ten Thousand Places* (Grand Rapids: Eerdmans, 2006), 1.

11. David E. Bjork, *Unfamiliar Paths: The Challenge of Recognizing the Work of Christ in Strange Clothing* (Pasadena, CA: William Carey Library, 1997).

12. Mother Columba Hart, Jane Bishop, and Barbara Newman, *Hildegard of Bingen: Scivias* (Mahwah, NJ: Paulist Press, 1990).

13. Father Richard Rohr wrote and posted this poem on the *Center for Action and Contemplation's* website, http://www.cacradicalgrace.org/resources/rg/2008/01_Apr-Jun/and.php. The final line reads, "And is why we are called the Center for Action AND Contemplation." Used with permission from the author.

Acknowledgments

If, as the saying goes, "it takes a village to raise a child," then surely it takes a network to write a book.

I am deeply grateful . . .

. . . for Mars Hill Graduate School; for its students who invite me to really show up, and in a special way for the students elected to take "The Kingdom of God and the New Sciences": Josué Blanco, Mark Closson, Richard Kim, Joshua Longbrake, Eric Nicolaysen, Tamara Renick, Scott Small, Kj Swanson, John Chandler, Austin Locklear, Philip Nellis, and Emily Thomas.

. . . for my colleagues Dan Allender, Bob Ekblad, Roy Barsness, Christie Lynk, Steve Call, Stephanie Neill, Chelle Stearns, O'Donnell Day, Caprice Hollins, and Keith Anderson, who have given me a place to belong and space to become.

. . . for the gracious people who made pastoring Quest: A Christ Commons such a glorious journey of exploration and for being a living lab of a networked church. Thank you.

. . . for Leonard Sweet and the cohort at George Fox University where many of these ideas first found words.

. . . for my loving family, Lynette and Pascal . . . for the Klassen family, Elvin and Sylvia; Bevan and Carolyn, Glendon, Steven and Jilaine . . . for the Friesen family, Ben and Roselle; Ken and Michelle, Shelby and Payton; Dallas and Leanne, and Josiah.

. . . for all my friends who read various versions of chapters, offering critical insight and warm encouragement. Roy Barsness, Cathy Loerzel, and especially Chelle Sterns, Todd Trembley, Jeff Cook, and Ron Carucci.

. . . for the many musicians whose compositions were my companions in writing. Special thanks to Sufjan Stevens, The Magnetic Fields, Jeff Johnson, Mozart, Augie March, Radiohead, Church of the Beloved, and Brian Eno.

. . . for the thoughtful research and writing of so many women and men who teach me to read, dare me to see, inspire me to hope, prompt me to think, and arouse me to live.

189

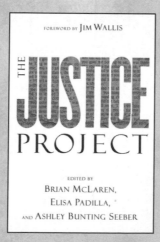

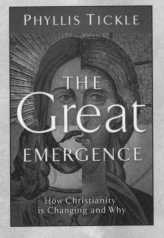
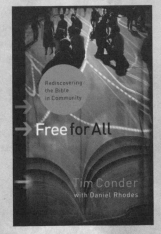